Spiritual Experiences and Revelations

Monica Koldyke Miller

Preface

This book came about because of my insatiable desire to read near-death experiences. I couldn't get enough of what happened to people, how they experienced God and who or what they encountered on 'the other side.' I was fascinated by this phenomena. Everything I learned reaffirmed what I believed about God the Father, Jesus and the Holy Spirit.

I recalled my own experiences where I'd felt divine intervention. Whenever I shared my stories, I discovered I wasn't alone. Many others also had spiritual experiences and their lessons always amazed me. And, if I could be uplifted and edified by these events, maybe others could too.

And so began my quest to find and then tell these stories. I've chosen stories with variety in mind as well as their universal and transformational qualities. I believe readers will easily relate to their struggles, doubts and fears.

I'm very grateful for the time, energy, and emotion it took for these wonderful people to share their stories. They sat through hours of taped interviews and endured endless follow up questions through multiple emails. I admire their bravery in exposing themselves to possible disbelief or ridicule. Nevertheless, each believed their story could help others in similar situations.

My desire is that these spiritual experiences give you hope, joy and new reasons to seek after God.

It has been a privilege to give each of them a voice.

Monica Koldyke Miller

This book is dedicated to those who feel lost, broken or forgotten.

"Therefore encourage one another and build each other up, just as in fact you are doing."

1Thessalonians 5:11

Contents

The Wakeup Call

We were late. We were afraid of getting into trouble. And so, as many teenagers do, my friend and I raced home to beat curfew. It had been raining all day and in fact was still drizzling at ten p.m. when we popped over a rise, our head-lights revealing water stretched across the road. Riding in my buddy's Mustang GT 5.0, we topped the hill at 85 miles an hour. I braced myself as my friend Forrest cut the wheel to the left, hitting the water without ever hitting the brakes. I became terrified when I felt the car's momentum go into the start of a roll...

...   .

An older sister, I and my twin brother were products of a broken home. We'd spent our first ten years living with an aunt and grandmother after our parents divorced. Dad, still a kid at heart, wasn't responsible enough to raise us. He'd visit on occasion, eating dinner and watching television, but never seemed to take seriously his role as parent. Because he wasn't a strong influence in our lives, we didn't care if he was there or not. Meanwhile, mom had remarried and moved to Japan to start another family.

Our aunt and grandmother became our parents. People used to call our aunt, our mother. When we got older, we stopped correcting them. Though they loved and took care of us, knowing we had a mother out there who didn't want us had taken its toll. We felt abandoned and unnoticed. Consequently, we hadn't developed a kinship of having a strong mother figure in our lives.

However, my brother and I had each other. We knew each other better than we knew ourselves. We shared everything. All the emotions we carried growing up, we carried together. We were literally and emotionally inseparable.

When our father remarried we went to live with him, gaining a step-mom and four step-siblings at once. We were ten years old. Despite our age, we knew we'd had a good thing going with our aunt and grandmother. They had done a lot for us, cared for us. We felt confused and a little bitter, knowing we were leaving them, our friends and school behind.

Our resentment grew when our older sister managed to act out just enough to return to our aunt and grandma's house. The best we could manage was to beg for frequent visits back to the only home we'd ever known. We would enjoy weekends here and there, two week visits during summer as well as trips they managed to provide. We'd go to SeaWorld and Kings Island, amusement parks in Ohio. We'd spend a week with them over Christmas break. When trips weren't possible, phone calls were the only connections we had.

Even though we lived with dad, his finances couldn't stretch for all our needs. When we wanted to get involved with sports, it was our aunt and grandma who provided money for equipment, clothes, shoes and allowances for our traveling basketball and baseball teams. We knew they loved us. It wasn't just the outward acts, but their affirmations of how much they missed us and wished we still lived with them. Those feelings were painfully mutual.

We learned to cope by staying away from our new home as much as possible. Since we didn't get along with our step-mom, we took every opportunity to stay with friends after school and weekends. By age eleven or twelve, video games and overnight stays with others became our norm.

Our life vividly changed from what we had known. Before, we went to church regularly, learning Bible stories. What we didn't learn at church, we learned from our aunt who was also a Sunday school teacher. Our new family, however, didn't belong to a church. In fact, they lived a lifestyle that many would consider rough. Six years later, my brother and I had adapted to this existence, turning away from our church-going ways.

It was at this time I began questioning whether God, or any of the stories I'd heard growing up were real. At sixteen, I no longer considered myself a church boy. Between my brother and myself, I wasn't the responsible one. Feelings of abandonment prodded me to act out to get noticed. I drank alcohol with friends. I smoked dope. I'd begun living a destructive lifestyle that had friends and family warning me, "If you keep this up, you're going to be in jail one day. You may not even graduate high school."

Is this how criminals start out? I wondered. I never responded to their warnings about finishing school. I didn't care about an education. I only went to see my friends. Why should I care when neither of my parents cared about me? Even our neighbors had to take us to get our driver's license.

And, if my parents didn't care, does that mean God doesn't care? Is God even *real?*

I had doubts. I had a lot of unanswered questions. The church I'd gone to as a child couldn't seem to answer them. So, I no longer considered myself a believer. How could I believe in something if I didn't know it even existed? For all I knew, religion was a practice people did to make themselves feel better.

The only thing I knew for sure; church people were boring!

There was however, one thing I was *very* interested in. Her name was Hannah. I had a crush on her, as did my twin brother. We were both very competitive and impressing her became another contest between us. The only way either of us could get to know her was to hang out at her house with a bunch of friends. In the process, we learned Hannah's father was pastor of a non-denominational church called Harvest Time Bible Church in Geneva, Indiana.

But it was Hannah's mom, Camelia Robles, who took an interest in my brother and me. Once she discovered our father had recently divorced again and we had no mother, she became our surrogate. She'd come over to do laundry, clean our house and many different things in order to know us better. She bought us Bibles and put them in our room. Before leaving from a day of cleaning, she'd open them to certain scriptures and place a book marker there. All the while, she'd call to check on us and ask if we were going to come to church. I could tell it was important to her and that she wanted us to get involved.

This is weird, I thought. Why would she have this much interest in us? Did she feel sorry for us? Did she see something in me, something she wanted to bring out that I didn't? I didn't understand. But, there was one thing I did know. I liked Hannah *a lot*. I liked her enough to go to their church.

For the next two months I went. I noticed the Robles were different from what I knew of churches and other church people. Camelia, who went by Cammy, was the embodiment of persistence. She often told me she was praying for me. And that wasn't the only thing different about the Robles or their church. This church played their music loud. To me, church music had always been an organ accompanying traditional hymnal songs. The music at Harvest Time was contemporary, new age. They had large subwoofers and a projection screen that displayed words to the songs. I'd never experienced church like this before. Additionally, they said they talked to God and God *talked back to them*. This blew away any type of traditional beliefs I had, because I thought praying meant repeating hundreds of times what you wanted and hopefully, something happens.

Yet, despite the fact I'd begun attending church; even though I had somebody reaching out to me, trying to connect with me and get me involved, it still didn't impact me enough. I was still undecided in my beliefs. I didn't know if any of it was real. I didn't know if I *wanted* to believe. And mostly, I didn't want to change my partying lifestyle. I was one of those kids that unless you could prove something to me, I didn't believe it.

And so, on a warm, rainy April night while racing to get home to beat curfew, God was the last thing on my mind.

The Mustang roared over the hill, headlights flashing onto water stretching the width of the road and approximately twelve feet in length. My buddy never took his foot off the gas and certainly had no time to hit the brakes. We slammed into water at 85 miles per hour as Forrest cut the wheel to the left. In the split second I felt the car begin its roll; I envisioned the car flipping several times.

I knew it was going be bad!

I braced, feeling the car's momentum propel itself sideways. Suddenly, an amazing thing happened. Rather than flipping, the Mustang began to hydroplane, spinning in circles. It spun five or six times in one spot, slowing as it went until it slid onto pavement on the other side. Once the car came out of the water, the friction of tire against asphalt again caused the car to feel as if it would roll over. Instead, it continued to spin, finally coming to a halt about forty feet away. We hadn't even left the road. At most, the nose of the car barely hung over the shoulder.

Both of us sat there, dazed, staring at each other. It had happened so fast I could scarce take it all in. The car hadn't flipped. It hadn't left the road. It was still running!

"Did you see that?" Forrest asked, finally. He put the car in gear and then began driving home s-l-o-w-l-y. "You know, I just—I just don't know," he said, shaking his head. "It felt like that was *it* for us. When I saw that water I was—I was just prepared to die."

"Yeah, I know what you mean," I said in agreement.

Forrest turned thoughtful. "You know, if heaven or hell is real, I don't think I would've gone to heaven."

"I'm in the same boat," I said. "I don't even know if I believe in any of this stuff."

The rest of the way home we tried reasoning between ourselves whether or not God was real. When I got home, I didn't tell my dad about the accident. I didn't want to scare him.

However, about twenty minutes after walking inside, the telephone rang. This was unusual. It was 2001. No one ever called at 10:30 at night. When I picked up the phone, it was Cammy, the pastor's wife. She said she had been anxious to talk with me.

"Oh, hello," I said. "Yeah, I'm sorry, I just got home."

"I've been praying for you these past couple of hours," she began.

"Is there anything I need to know?" I asked.

"Has anything happened recently? Yesterday, or today?"

My interest immediately piqued. "Uh, well, what do you mean *recently?* What exactly do you mean by that?"

"I don't know. Anytime during the last day or today even; did you feel like your life was in danger?"

Suddenly, I could feel my heart beating rapidly as emotion choked my throat. Had Forrest called my brother? Had my brother called Cammy? Yet, I knew there hadn't been time. *I'd just gotten home.* "What do you mean? What are you getting at?" I finally managed to say.

"Well, I'd been praying for you," she said, "and God showed me that Satan was going to try to take your life." My jaw dropped as she continued. "But, God told me that He was going to intervene, because He has a plan for you. He has a purpose for your life. He's not going to let Satan steal that."

I couldn't believe what I was hearing. I was speechless. *How could she know?* I knew exactly what she was talking about for it had just happened.

"Were you—did you just get into an accident?" she said, persistently. "Did anything like that happen?"

"T-thank you for praying for me," I said, sputtering. "I need—I need to go!" I hung up, too upset to talk. The situation had suddenly become very, very real.

I had a lot to think about.

I went to my room knowing there was no way she could've known what happened except by how she described. This realization blew my mind. I had to make a decision. *Had I really been targeted by dark forces?* This was my life! And yet, I'd been shown it could be taken away at any time.

I'd become very nonchalant about choosing faith. I was now scared at how close I had come to losing that chance. Could I live with the uncertainty of not knowing whether I'd go to a good or awful place when I died?

It had to be true. *God must be real!*

That very night I made my choice. I chose to believe. I decided that if something like that ever happened to me again,

I wasn't going to have to worry. So, I did what everybody had told me to do, what I'd heard in church a million times. I confessed to God that I was a sinner. I asked Him to forgive my sins. I believed Jesus came and died for those sins and He rose from the grave. I believed His death paid for my sins.

Immediately, immense feelings of love and acceptance washed over me. Not only that, but feelings of being *chosen*. God didn't care what I'd done. Nor, did He condemn me for my doubts. His 'judge-free' love fell on me like a blanket and all I could do was weep. God had a plan and purpose for my life! I wanted to find out what that plan and purpose was.

I changed from that point on.

I called Camelia the very next day. "Hey, I just have to let you know about last night. At first, I thought you'd talked to someone and were playing a joke on me."

She assured me she hadn't spoken to anyone. However, I wanted to be sure. "Are you sure you didn't talk to anyone about what happened last night?"

"No, I was just curious. I felt like something was happening and wanted to make you aware of what was going on while I prayed for you."

I decided to tell her about my experience. She didn't seem surprised at all. "I *knew* something like that was going to happen! Are you now going to get serious about coming to church?" Always the closer, Cammy reinforced my decision. "Well, you need to come back to church, then," she said, insisting.

And, so I did. I came to believe God used that night to reach out to me; to answer my questions. I think He intervened early in my life because of the destructive path I'd been traveling. Otherwise, I could've lost my soul.

It felt intimidating to be on Satan's radar. He'd seen the influence the Robles had on my life and where I was heading. I believe he wanted to keep that from happening.

That night, I confided with my brother what had happened. Amazingly, he wasn't surprised. He'd had experiences that already prodded him toward a relationship with God. "I think it's time we both got serious about God," he said. "I've already committed myself, and so should you."

The experience caused me to value life even more. I felt a renewed sense of gratitude for those around me and for those who'd prayed for me. I also didn't want to see my friends die and go to hell. I wanted to share my story with them. As I did, it continued to impact me.

As a result of this experience, I grew to love the Lord and studied His word. I got really deep into church. A year or two later, I felt a calling to ministry. And, so in 2010 I moved to Cleveland, Tennessee and attended New Life Bible College, obtaining a degree in theology and Christian ministry. I'm not pastoring a church now, but it's my intention to eventually become pastor of a church.

And if you're curious, no, I didn't get the girl! My twin brother ended up dating Hannah throughout high school. Thankfully, we've always viewed competition as a way of bringing out the best in each other. Whether work related, athletics or love interests, we've never been competitive on a level that caused either of us to be angry or upset with the other.

Looking back, I now believe Satan wanted to kill me because he could see if I continued to be mentored by the Robles, I'd discover my calling. That discovery would ultimately disrupt his kingdom order, his army, which is in conflict with Christ's kingdom. He knew my changed life would impact others and I think he saw me as a threat. I'm very thankful God prevented Satan from stealing my life and more importantly, my salvation.

I now realize that God loved me from the very beginning. He loved me enough to provide the kind of mother I needed despite the women my father chose. It wasn't just Cammy's plan to reach out to save a life; save a soul for the kingdom. It was God stretching out His hand *through* her, to mend my brokenness despite my imperfections.

When my aunt got married and moved away, I was fifteen. Cammi Robles came into my life soon after, picking up where my aunt had left off. The first I called mom, the second *ma*.

When people asked why I called Cammy that, I'd explain she's our *Christian* mom. We ate many Thanksgivings with her. We spent many Christmas's with her, receiving just as many gifts as her other children. Her unrelenting commitment taught us how to receive love. She became the guide that showed us the changing factor in our life was Jesus. And just like Jesus, she wouldn't let us go in the wrong direction.

My brother and I had grown up feeling rejected. Unwanted. With our birth mom leaving and dad always absent even after moving in with him, we believed ourselves unworthy. It was then that God revealed Himself to us through the Robles. I'm so thankful for His grace which protected me that night and covered my sins for life. He took something that could've been very bad, losing my life, and turned it around. In the process He revealed Himself. I believed He loved me and had a plan, saying, *"I'm real and I'm here."*

That gave me hope, peace and excitement for my future.

As it says in the Bible, *"As it is written, 'I have made you the father of many nations.' Abraham acted in faith when he stood in the presence of God, who gives life to the dead and calls into existence things that don't yet exist."* (Romans 4:17)

When Cammy shared this with me, it resonated.

Even when teachers or family saw me as a future criminal, God sees me completely different. She explained, "God gives life to the dead. He quickens the dead. He can take something that's dead and give it life." She went even further, "God calls you righteous. He calls you faithful. He calls you blessed."

That meant I wasn't hopeless. I was salvageable. Jesus had redeemed me from death to life.

Chris Merchant
Decatur, Indiana

Footnote: Though it's been several years since that fateful event, my buddy and I still marvel that we've still never seen standing water in that particular place, either before or afterward. It's an area of road that never floods**...**

Forgiven

"I'm pregnant."

I stood stock still, my back to my parents. I couldn't bear to face them. How had I gotten to this point? I'd been raised in a loving family, attended church and had accepted Christ at a young age. Living in the small community of Berne, Indiana however, had its own set of issues. You're bound to be associated by whom your parents and grandparents were, and even your siblings. Despite knowing otherwise, I lacked certainty that I fit in.

I constantly felt compared to my older, more accomplished sister. I wasn't as talented. I wasn't as good of a student. She seemed perfect while I couldn't quite measure up. Though never spoken, I felt the pressure of everyone's expectations based on my sister's abilities.

As a consequence of my own insecurities, I began to fall away from God. Since I didn't feel I'd ever be as good as my sister, I decided to do whatever I wanted. Rules were for them, not me. I took up drinking and partying. I bought into the lie that sex wasn't that big of a deal. That's what you did when you were in a relationship. Ultimately, my conviction to remain pure before marriage tumbled out of favor.

Being a people-pleaser, I didn't have the confidence to stand up for convictions I knew deep down were true. I thought so little of myself that when I began dating a boy outside my social group, I foolishly went along with anything he wanted. I had become the good girl who went astray. Within a month of becoming physical, I *knew* I was pregnant.

I was seventeen. I felt scared and didn't know what to do. Suddenly, a thought shot across my mind. *You could end this pregnancy and no one would ever have to know.*

Where had that idea come from? I'd been raised to know abortion ended a human life. A part of my deeply ingrained beliefs rose to the fore. And just as fast as the thought flashed through my mind, I answered back with a resounding *No!* I knew I couldn't do something like that.

Being scared and ashamed, I prolonged telling anyone of my condition. But God had His own way of forcing out the truth. That year, a measles outbreak in the Amish community caused the state health department to require booster vaccinations of all students. Due to a Health Occupations class I was taking, I had enough common sense to realize it wasn't a good idea to be vaccinated while pregnant.

Gathering courage, I broached the subject with a nurse during my clinical rotation in the ER at Adams Memorial Hospital. The morning was slow and I was sitting with her in the nurse's station. "If someone thinks they're pregnant, they probably shouldn't get the measles vaccine, right?"

"No," she said, before looking right at me. "Why, do you think you're pregnant?"

When I told her I thought I was, she stated I needed a pregnancy test. She took me into an exam room where the doctor soon ordered a test, telling me to come back for the results after school. I returned with a friend later that day, but the doctor was no longer on duty. He was kind enough to have me come to his house so that he could share privately that the results were indeed positive. He wrote me a doctor's excuse stating that due to pregnancy, I wasn't to receive the measles vaccine scheduled the next day.

With the measles outbreak, the requirement from the Health Department was that you either had to receive the booster shot or you had to miss two weeks of school. I now hoped the doctor's note would clear me of that consequence, allowing me to keep my secret a bit longer.

My plan for avoiding the issue backfired however, when the nurse, after reading the note asked me if my parents knew. When I replied that they didn't, she marched me to the principles office to inform him why I couldn't receive the vaccine. "Well, I guess they're going to find out now," she said tartly.

When I returned to class, it was obvious by my tearful look that something was wrong. At one point between classes, while at my locker, the girl next to me asked if getting the booster shot had been very bad. When I told her I didn't get it, she asked in a loud voice, "Why, are you pregnant?"

I could've crawled into my locker. "Be more quiet," I murmured, feeling everyone's eyes swing my direction.

Looking concerned, she lowered her voice. "I can take you to Indianapolis for an abortion," she whispered. "I've gone with someone before."

I recalled that her idea had been presented to me once before. It felt as if Satan was once again trying to get me to succumb to his schemes. "I'm not interested," I said, shutting my locker door. I knew having an abortion would only make this problem temporarily go away; but a person would have to live with that decision forever. I stubbornly refused. I didn't want any part of it.

A glimmer of hope arose when I later discovered a way out of my two-week suspension. If I could prove I'd already received two vaccinations for measles, I didn't need a booster. I returned the very next day with my immunization records and had my suspension reversed.

But the damage had already been done. As small towns go, rumors began to fly. Within days, I received a phone call from my older sister. She said she'd heard gossip about me being pregnant and wanted to know if it was true.

Being the era of corded phones and located in the living room, I tried being vague and discreet as our mom kept walking past me.

At first, silence met my cryptic confirmation. "Make up an excuse to not come to lunch on Sunday," she said, referring to our parent's planned anniversary meal. "I won't be able to pretend everything is normal."

I promised I would.

That Sunday was the longest day of my life. I stayed at a friend's house, fretting. What was happening? Would my sister betray me? What would they say? My emotions undulated like a roller coaster, one minute scared my sister would tell, the next, relieved I wouldn't be the one to confess.

Finally, the phone rang. It was my mom, asking when I'd be home. "I'm coming home now," I responded. After hanging up, my friend hugged me and sent me on my way. When I walked in, my parents were waiting. Fearfully, I asked how dinner went and what my sister may have told them.

"She said we needed to talk. That you had something to tell us."

The moment of truth had come. I couldn't put it off anymore. In one short week my life had fallen to pieces. I proceeded to walk through the family room and into the kitchen. I stopped, keeping my back to my parents. Nervous and scared, I couldn't bring myself to face them.

"I'm pregnant," I blurted out.

I could hear mom crying. Fearing his reaction, I looked toward dad, knowing how disappointed he must feel. And yet, he stood waiting with tears running down his face, his arms wide open.

I had a sudden image of God the Father waiting with open arms and unconditional love; waiting patiently for me to come to Him.

With immense relief, I felt truly *forgiven*. Though I had always known that they loved me, it never before felt so real. I immediately rushed to him, weeping as he enveloped me.

I knew my life had been forever changed by the choices and decisions I'd made. That night was a turning point. It wasn't just about me anymore. It was about the life growing inside me.

My family, church and mentors came together, encouraging and giving support where ever they could. Through their efforts I found the strength to prepare for this new chapter in my life. Two women in particular, my youth pastor's wife and another youth volunteer, drove me and another girl for parenting classes in Fort Wayne, a city almost an hour away.

As there were no alternatives, they began questioning the need for this type of resource in our own community. That began a vision of what was then The Hope Center which has now evolved into The Hope Clinic, serving clients in both Berne and (nearby) Decatur areas. Their mission is to give hope while striving to be the first choice for those in the midst of an unplanned pregnancy. By offering support for both men and women, providing material needs and education as well as compassionate care, they've helped hundreds in Adams County in situations like mine.

It's now been twenty-five years since that fateful day. I went on to graduate high school before earning an RN degree. I'm married with a family and a daughter I can't imagine living without. I feel as if I have come full circle, having now served on the Hope Clinic Board for the past five years. I've since realized if Satan tried to disillusion and tempt me, a believer, what about those who don't believe or know the truth of God's love? How can I not be that source of hope and light?

Because of Christ and His forgiveness, I'm now able to give back. It's become my calling to serve those who like me, felt the desperation of an unplanned pregnancy.

I'm reminded of God's love and forgiveness daily. His Word gives me the strength to do what I do. The verses that mean the most to me are:

"Imitate God, therefore, in everything you do, because you are his dear children. Live a life filled with love, following the example of Christ. He loved us and offered himself as a sacrifice for us, a pleasing aroma to God." Ephesians 5: 1-2 New Living Translation

"For God has not given us a spirit of fear and timidity, but of power, love and self-discipline." 2 Timothy 1: 7 New Living Translation

"And may you have the power to understand, as all God's people should, how wide, how long, how high, and how deep is his love." Ephesians 3: 18

Lesley Hough
Berne, Indiana

The Skin of Jesus

"And a woman was there who had been subject to bleeding for twelve years. She had suffered a great deal under the care of many doctors and had spent all she had, yet instead of getting better she grew worse. When she heard about Jesus, she came up behind him in the crowd and touched his cloak, because she thought, "If I just touch his clothes, I will be healed." Immediately her bleeding stopped and she felt in her body that she was freed from her suffering." Mark 5: 26-29

The Appalachian city of Blaine, tucked in the back hills of Kentucky was looked upon as home to 250 souls the summer of 2009. Our family of four as well as one other member of our Lutheran church had traveled over three hundred miles to help with several construction projects for Blaine Christian Church and Outreach. Head minister of the little country church, Pastor Lenny, had just shared Proverbs 3: 5-6 in the prayer service on the last day of our mission trip. Filled three-quarters to capacity, the sanctuary held over one hundred people.

"Trust in the Lord with all your heart and lean not on your own understanding; in all your ways acknowledge him, and he will make your paths straight."

At the end of the service, he looked over the packed congregation. "Anyone in need of healing and desiring prayer, please join us at the front of the church."

I sat glued to my seat. I thought to myself, *There's no way I can go up there*! However, my husband, John, kept looking at me, prodding me with his eyes. At this point in my life, I'd not been feeling well. In fact, I'd been ill for many years.

In the past, I'd always been able to fix things. Control things. Yet, this illness had defied my efforts, leaving me confused hurt and frustrated. And, deep down; afraid. If only I could work harder. Learn more about my disease. *Fix myself.*

Suddenly, I felt the tugging of the Holy Spirit. It's not the first time I'd experienced His presence. I recognized the feeling as well as His calm and peaceful voice. *Susan, now is the time. It's time for you to stop.* It was almost as if I heard the words in my head. I felt John touch my arm. Though unspoken, his intent seemed clear. *You need to do this.*

In my weakness, my heart rebelled. *I've been at this for a long time, Lord. I've prayed! I've had others pray over me. This hasn't worked before. Why would it now?* And though I couldn't admit it, I didn't trust I'd be healed.

I thought it would take everything I had within me to get up and move forward. I stood up, almost as if someone had lifted me and then took me toward the front. My heart and mind felt the Lord saying words of comfort; *I'm leading you here because this is where I need you to be.*

All at once, my fear was gone. I felt warm, comforted. I was in good hands. Nothing would harm me; this was intended for my good.

...   .

In the spring of 1997, I was pregnant with my first son, David. I developed an infection called C.diff. When something upsets the normal balance of microorganisms in your digestive tract, bacteria can grow out of control and make you sick. One of the worst offenders is a bacterium called *Clostridium difficile*, or C.diff. As bacteria overgrow, they release toxins that attack the lining of the intestines. Though relatively rare, this type of infection can range from mild to life threatening.

After the initial infection cleared up, I continued to have issues which led to further gastrointestinal troubles. This continued over a long time and eventually I was diagnosed with ulcerative proctitis. For anyone who's ever suffered with any kind of bowel disease, one of the most difficult things is; you look healthy on the outside, but what's going on in the *inside* is very painful. Furthermore, my internal distress wasn't evident to others.

For a while, symptoms were minimal. Occasionally, there'd be flare-ups, yet I could control them with diet and medication. However, during the summer of 2008 my latest flare refused to abate. A colonoscopy showed that my disease had not progressed, but in an attempt to lessen my symptoms, my physician started me on a different medication. I became increasingly ill. I'd never been a big person; always a normal weight. Now, I began losing weight. No matter what I ate, nourishment went right through me. The ulcerations in my colon were causing bloody diarrhea up to fifteen times a day, causing my hemoglobin to drop leaving me feeling weak.

During this time, I was trying to balance going to nursing school with a husband who worked full time as well as two school-age children. I was in the midst of an intense summer nursing class when my body plunged out of remission.

Despite all this, I didn't recognize *how* sick I really was.

John and I were discussing this right before he was to take the boys on a camping trip. "Maybe, you should go see the doctor," he said.

"I've called them over and over about this. If I go in, they're just going to tell me what they've already said before. Nothing's going to change."

However, I finally gave in and made an appointment the day they left on their trip. My weight had recently fallen to a hundred pounds. I looked gaunt. People were noticing. *Ok, Lord. I've done everything! I've tried every diet under the sun, I've eliminated foods, and I'm hardly eating. I don't know what else to do.* And, so I went.

"Well," the doctor said, reviewing my chart, "I want to put you in the hospital."

I shook my head. "No, I can't. My husband's out of town."

"It'll just be for the weekend, I promise."

"Can't we do this at home?" I asked hesitantly. I didn't want to be hospitalized.

"I *really* think you need to do this."

I don't know if it was the tone of his voice or if I'd just grown weary, but I finally said, "Okay."

"It'll just be a weekend," he said, trying to assure me. "I'll put you in the hospital and we'll get this under control."

I started feeling better the moment they put me on steroids. Yet, the doctors at the hospital wanted another colonoscopy. I reluctantly agreed, thinking I'd gotten through the worst of it.

I was wrong.

The colonoscopy revealed my entire colon had become severely inflamed. I'd developed full blown ulcerative colitis and was hospitalized fourteen days. John had returned from the camping trip by the time I received this news.

"Had you not come into the hospital, you could have gone septic," the doctor explained. "Not only would you have lost your colon, but you could've lost your life."

I stared at the doctor in shock. How could this be? It was the lowest time of my life.

In the past, I'd heard other people explain how they had found Christ. How they'd suffered abuse in childhood or that things hadn't gone well, and how the Lord had turned their life around. I, on the other hand, never had a testimony like that to tell.

I'd always felt blessed to have grown up with loving parents and in a Christian home. I married an equally loving husband and had healthy, beautiful children. Now, for the first time in my life, to lose my health; I couldn't figure out what was going on. I even begged for answers. *Lord, I've done everything I've been called to do. I'm faithful in worship, prayer and Bible study. Why is this happening to me?*

Since college, I'd journaled off and on to channel my emotions. But, it wasn't until my illness that it became my daily companion. From my hospital bed, I wrote these words:

July 26, 2008
In Psalm 13, David wrote, 'How long, O Lord? Will you forget me forever? How long will you hide your face from me? How long must I wrestle with my thoughts and every day have sorrow in my heart? How long will my enemies triumph over me?'

Like David, I have been feeling forgotten. I feel like this enemy called ulcerative colitis is being allowed to have its way with my body. It feels as though all my efforts to conquer it are fruitless. Nothing I am doing seems to matter at all—the diet—the journaling—the scripture reading—the medication—

the prayer, nothing changes. I am still not sleeping, I still wake up in pain. I am cramped, bleeding, fatigued, depressed, and angry.

How long O Lord? How long must I live like this? Why am I not getting better? What am I doing wrong? Where is my sin? Am I being punished? When will it stop?

Oh Lord, you are the only one who can change this, who can heal me. I beg of you Lord, please show mercy and heal me. Please take this away. Please make me whole—physically, spiritually, and mentally. I feel so broken. I feel so out of control. I need you to heal me.

David said 'Look on me and answer, O Lord my God. Give light to my eyes or I will sleep in death, my enemy will say "I have overcome him and my foes will rejoice when I fall."

Lord, I don't want to give in, I want to heal. I want to be whole. David felt your protection—he said "But I trust in your unfailing love; my heart rejoices in your salvation. I will sing to the Lord for he has been good to me."

Lord I want to feel that love. I know you are there—but you feel so far away. Peace and contentment are so hard to find right now. In my head I know how good you are to me, I just need to feel it in my heart too. Please Lord, help me to see what David saw and bring peace to my troubled soul.

Over the next several months my body began to heal. For me however, it was the beginning of a dawning realization. Though difficult to accept, my illness had forced me to face a *spiritual* reality. My stubborn insistence in fixing my wellbeing on my own had failed. And, I would never find true peace until I yielded control of my health to Him.

I began to see that God was building a testimony for me.

Though I'd returned home with a minimum of health, weakness during my recovery period made it difficult to take care of the kids. I felt dismayed at limitations I now had, like finding myself out of breath walking from car to baseball field. Often, I felt too weak to perform routine household duties.

A few weeks later after my release from the hospital, I wrote this in my journal.

September 6, 2008
Psalm 119: 18-19 "Open my eyes that I may see wonderful things in your law. I am a stranger on earth; do not hide your commands from me."

The idea of being a stranger here on earth makes so much sense to me. I can't say that I feel it all the time—but there are times when longing for heaven comes upon me. I wish I could say the longing is in every situation—but it is usually when things are difficult. The human side of me struggles with the desire to be wife, mom, friend, nurse, and possibly mission-ary here on earth for many years to come. Then, every once in awhile, I feel the Holy Spirit reminding me that I am living for eternity.

During this illness, I feel as though God is building a testimo-ny for me to be able to share with others more easily and purposefully. I look at this earthly body and feel frustrated with its weakness and ugliness. It is not what God intended— He intended perfection. The psalmist says in verse 20, "my soul is consumed with longing for our laws at all times." I wonder how it feels to be consumed like that. I often feel more like Paul in my struggle to do what God commands. The desire is there, but I allow myself to do the sins I want to avoid.

The psalmist has this all consuming passion to live for God I pray that the Holy Spirit begins to develop in me a passion— not just for God's commands, but for God and eternity. I know that it is purely God's grace that saves me regardless of my ability to keep or break his commands. I just pray that through developing in my faith I can become more passionate and open with others in my walk here. We all need to be strangers on this earth—because heaven is our only home.

You'd think I would've learned my lesson. But, I didn't! As I healed, which took several months, I went back to nursing school. I was now in remission. I felt better. But, because I'd missed a semester, I pushed hard in my studies. Some of my old habits crept back. I allowed stress to find its way back in and I sought to control school, home and family. My relationship with God had changed, but I struggled with my old self. I struggled to allow Him to be in control.

And, once again, I became ill.

I started bleeding again, and heavily. This continued even though my doctor had been making adjustments to my medications.

Ironically, it was almost exactly a year from the time I'd been deathly sick. Doubly ironic, was the fact that a year ago my family had been preparing to go on a mission trip. And, that mission trip had been postponed a year. At the time, I was thinking, "Well, that's all right, in a year I'll be healthy and things will be okay."

And, here I was, sick again right before I was to leave. I saw my doctor and told him, "I'm supposed to go on this mission trip and I really think God's calling me to go."

"You'd be foolish," he said. "What are you going to do if you get sick? Do you even know if there's a hospital nearby?"

"I don't know, but I believe God will take care of me," I said with confidence.

However, my words didn't match my convictions. Though I had people praying over me, my heart still struggled with completely trusting God and whether this was the right thing to do. I felt weak. My hemoglobin had dropped again, causing fatigue. All the way to Blaine, I sat in the back of the van chiding myself silently. *What are you doing?* I thought. *You're such a stupid girl!*

When we first arrived, the church held a prayer service to welcome the mission teams. Having grown up in a Lutheran church, I was accustomed to a conservative style of worship. There's not a lot of stomping, hand raising or jumping around. There's definitely not a lot of emotional prayer and praying over people during worship.

On that very first night in this little country church, the wife of a guest preacher rose to pray over people in the congregation. As she walked around the sanctuary praying for people, I sat quietly with my family. She approached me and said, "There's something wrong. I believe you're in need of prayer." She raised her hand and prayed that God would come to me and bring healing for what I needed.

I sat there, thinking, *How did she know that?* My biggest struggle had been always looking healthy outside, but hurting inside. I had become accustomed to strangers being unaware of my illness. Not knowing what to think, I let it go.

Soon, everyone found a job to do. A floor needed to be laid, the outside of the church needed paint as well as other, general church maintenance. Yet due to my weakness, I needed to discuss things with Pastor Lenny. "I'm not totally healthy. I'm not being lazy, but I won't be able to do the physical work that you need done."

"That's okay," he said. "We're also putting together a vacation Bible school."

"That's perfect!" I said, thrilled. "I was once a teacher. I've put together many programs in my church." And, so I was able to sit quietly but be extremely helpful in painting and putting together set work for plays as well as Bible lessons.

As the week progressed, I kept seeing people who had so little yet were so open, so gracious in their faith and willing to share with others. Humble and gentle, they weren't preoccupied with what others thought. But, it was obvious to me they were filled with the Holy Spirit as they worked to enrich God's kingdom. Being amongst them filled me with joy.

Towards the end of the week, the very last night, there was another prayer service. That night, the church was full of people. People I didn't know. Perfect strangers. I'd gotten to know a few, but not like those in my own church.

While not something to which I was accustomed, I understood the practice of laying on of hands and anointing of oil as described in Scripture. However, I'd never experienced it myself. It wasn't common practice in my church and if it was done at all, it was done privately.

So why was I afraid to allow myself to be a part of something that God had given directions to the early church to do? I think at that point, I was so low; I was spiritually struggling. And so it was less admitting I had a weakness but more acknowledging my lack of trust that God would heal me through this type of venue.

While in nursing school, I'd done endless research on Irritable Bowel diseases, Crohn's and colitis. I was of the belief; people aren't just healed from these diseases. And yet, Pastor Lenny had told me earlier in the week, "Susan, the Lord's healed me from Crohn's disease."

My internal response had been *Well, maybe, but how do you know for sure?*

Could I truly believe him? God hadn't healed me. But, the more I got to know Pastor Lenny and saw God working in and through him; it felt like a light bulb had been turned on. For the first time, I believed God *had* healed someone and it was a disease very similar to my own.

Lenny believed it. And, he told me he'd been healed after being anointed with oil. I had thought of this often throughout the week, and now he was asking me to trust him and step out in faith.

"Anyone in need of healing and desiring prayer, please join us at the front of the church."

Two other people besides me responded to Pastor Lenny's request. As I stood there, Pastor Jerry, Lenny's associate prayed over me. Both pastors placed hands on my head and shoulders as Jerry prayed. "Please bring healing to this woman from her current suffering," he said out loud. "And, restore her body to health. Please correct the disorders of her blood and may it return to normal." Additionally, he prayed about my blood counts and private conversations I'd had with my doctor on the phone. Then, Lenny dipped his finger into a small jar of olive oil and anointed my head.

I was astounded by his words and became very emotional. Pastor Jerry had not been at the church all week, arriving shortly before the prayer service. No one had told him of my health problems. How could he know so much about me when he didn't even know me? It had to have been the Holy Spirit, which gave him insight.

Romans 8: 26 flashed through my mind. *"In the same way the Spirit helps us in our weakness. We do not know what we ought to pray for, but the Spirit himself intercedes for us with groans that words cannot express."*

I suddenly thought, *"The Holy Spirit didn't just intercede for me with groans and inexpressible words, but he also put words in this man's mouth!"*

With a certainty I'd never before known, the Lord revealed to me He alone had the power to direct my life. God had a better plan and my first and last job was *to trust* Him with it.

I finally let go.

I'd always tried overcoming life's challenges by my own power and strength. I struggled with God's sovereignty; not only in my life, but the whole universe as well. *If* I found healing, it'd only be through His efforts, not mine. For the first time in my life, I fully submitted my illness to the Lord.

The very next day, I read again Proverbs 3: 5-6. However, I didn't stop at the sixth verse. I read the next two verses. *"Do not be wise in your own eyes; fear the Lord and shun evil. This will bring health to your body and nourishment to your bones."*

Even though I knew God had healed me, it wasn't until that moment, as I read the passage again, that I recognized exactly what God had accomplished. It was at that moment I knew I had stopped bleeding. I was overwhelmed and filled with joy!

For so long I'd been relying on my own wisdom. I'd always believed there had to be something *I could do* to heal my colon. But, that wasn't what God wanted me to do. As Hebrews 12: 1-3 entered my mind; it became another reminder of where my focus should be. I needed to fix my eyes on Him and not be caught up in the things of the world. The concept about living for eternity rather than for today, really hit home.

I then made this entry in my journal:

July 3, 2009 Blaine Mission Trip, Day 5

Proverbs 3: 5-8 "Trust in the Lord with all your heart and lean not on your own understanding; in all your ways acknowledge him, and he will make your paths straight. Do not be wise in your own eyes; fear the Lord and shun evil. This will bring health to your body and nourishment to your bones."

Last night I found healing here in Blaine. I stood before God in a church full of strangers and asked two men to pray over my body, anoint me, and plead with God to heal me. While I felt scared, embarrassed, and overwhelmed, I also felt the Spirit leading me to embrace that moment. I am so humbled by these sweet, kind, caring, gentle mountain people who wear the skin of Jesus. For so long I have been trusting on my own understanding, searching for cures and answers as to what I could do to bring healing to my body. During this past week, God has shown me that it is foolishness to believe that I can do anything. God alone will heal when and if He chooses to heal me.

As I listened to Pastor Jerry Sparks pray over me last night, I was amazed by the words given to him. It was as if he knew my disease personally. In my conservative, reserved traditional way of worship and prayer, I have never been as bold for another as he was last night. How beautiful this simple, straight-forward anointing this man did. He totally trusts that the Lord will heal me. He confidently made my requests known and placed me in the arms of Jesus.

Pastor Lenny Wheeler is an amazing man. No one I have ever known exemplifies Proverbs 3 like Lenny. He trusts completely that the Lord will not only meet his every need, but the needs of everyone else around him. Lenny has spiritual wisdom beyond any of the sophisticated, learned men I know, because he simply trusts what the Bible says and does it. I pray that I can find that kind of trust. He knows first hand the pain of IBS (Irritable Bowel Syndrome) because he suffered with Crohn's (Disease). It would be easy, by worldly wisdom, to say that he is just in remission. But, I believe God has healed Lenny to work in his kingdom. If Lenny had not had Crohn's, it would have been difficult for me to walk up last night.

I still have a long way to go in trusting the Lord completely. I am discovering that it is an area of weakness greater than I ever realized. For today, I trust that the Lord has begun to work healing in my body. I need to stop spending so much time worrying about what to eat and what not to eat, what to do and what not to do, and just seek Him.

In the morning when I rise,
In the morning when I rise,
In the morning when I rise,
 Give me Jesus.

I've come to understand many things through my hardship of ill health. Two things stand in the forefront. Trusting in the Lord and overcoming my pride. It took Him taking me to the point of extreme illness before I recognized that I was not in control. He is. God controls my life as well as my health.

The hardest thing for me had been asking others to help with things I had deemed my job. In a woman's world that means taking care of her vocation; her family; her children. That's where my pride had pushed God's grace away. How could I not handle what I'd always handled before? With my do-it-yourself attitude, I couldn't see that He wanted to show me His love and strength *through my weakness.*

His desire is that I be in relationship with Him. That I be transformed. That, that renewing of my mind continues. Knowing that I cannot control everything is what I've really learned from this. I've also learned the importance of leaning on the Lord and trusting in Him.

Before, it was all about what I was doing. I always focused on me. I relied on my own wisdom. I believed with enough effort, I could heal my colon. All the while, I wasn't focused on what God was doing through me.

When sharing my experience with others, I'm careful to include one last thought. I'm not saying that if they let go and put everything in God's hands that all the problems of this world or their life will go away. The Lord never promises His children wouldn't have trouble or disease. People everywhere are suffering with issues from which they may never recover. It's just that He often allows hardships for His purposes.

Even now, I cling to Hebrews 12: 1-3. *"Therefore, since we are surrounded by such a great cloud of witnesses, let us throw off everything that hinders and the sins that so easily entangles, and let us run with perseverance the race marked out for us Let us fix our eyes on Jesus, the author and perfecter of our faith, who for the joy set before him endured the cross, scorning its shame and sat down at the right hand of the throne of God. Consider him who endured such opposition from sinful men, so that you will not grow weary and lose heart."*

What had been hurting on the inside wasn't just my illness. It was my unbelief. Jesus, through the Holy Spirit, healed both. Through this experience, I now realize that transformation even occurs for those who already know Christ as their Savior. Learning to lean on Him through difficult times was also a witness of faith.

And, though I couldn't reach out to touch Jesus' robe, He touched me through the hands of his children, healing my own twelve year disease.

I now had my testimony!

Susan Hein
Fort Wayne, Indiana

Comatose

Tears filled my eyes as I walked down the aisle toward the prayer area at my church in West Palm Beach, Florida. I had just buried my seventeen year old daughter after she had been in a coma for nearly a week. My prayer life, which had always included prayers for my family, often ended with "God, don't let the devil eat my children." The quote came about from asking God to protect them. I believed 1 Peter 5:8 when it said, "Your enemy the devil prowls around like a roaring lion looking for someone to devour."

As I knelt down to pray, I thought, *Well, God, it looks like you let the devil eat one!*

... ...

Dawneva Aubrey Hicks had been a troubled child. Lying and skipping school had been the least of her problems. Six months prior, she'd been diagnosed with clinical depression and had been prescribed a strong antidepressant. She had even been admitted to a mental hospital. After four months the insurance ran out. She had been dismissed without having made any progress. Dawn had become so out of control, it was decided that she should reside somewhere other than our home. The decision was not difficult. More than anything, my wife and I wanted what was best for her. She then began living with one of her high school teachers while continuing outpatient therapy. Unfortunately, this arrangement did not stop her downward spiral the few weeks she stayed there.

Tuesday, May 21, 1988, Dawn had been caught skipping school once again. During the confrontation her teacher told her she was in trouble and that she would have to go *home*. Possibly, to divert the consequences of her behavior, Dawn took a small overdose of antidepressants. Knowing she had a scheduled outpatient counseling session that evening led us to believe she intended to only get sick from taking extra medication. However, upon arriving at the hospital, she soon went into a seizure. She didn't realize her medicine was dangerous because the label warning had simply stated 'Caution, may cause drowsiness.' She wouldn't know that even though doctors pumped her stomach and gave her a pace-maker to keep her heart pumping, she'd soon be declared brain-dead. She only knew she was *in trouble. Trouble* meant going back to her real home. She did not want to go home to the religious cult her family had been involved with for twelve years.

My life had been no less troubled than my daughter's. As a teen, I'd perpetrated breaking and entering crimes, accumulated speeding violations and had been arrested and jailed for drunk-driving by age sixteen. With a phony driver's license and no father to guide me, I had drifted from one meaningless endeavor to another. When grown, I lived a hippie lifestyle which included smoking pot and trying LSD.

I didn't know what I sought, but looked for it in drugs, reckless living and communal relationships. Eventually, I realized it was God I needed, but searched in all the wrong places. I had become a member of a religious cult where independent thinking was prohibited and blind obedience was demanded. My one saving grace was my active prayer life. No matter the circumstance, I loved God and I knew He loved me.

Now, in the hospital, my daughter lay in a coma. I'd been assured the doctors had done everything they could, but there was no cure for this type of seizure. Dawn had slipped away without my being able to say goodbye. My Dawny was gone! There was nothing else to do except take her off life support.

Soon, a team of doctors from the University of Miami came to discuss the possibility of organ donation. They explained what a benefit it would be to others since Dawn was young, healthy and a non-smoker. I agreed. That night, I brought in her two younger sisters and younger brother for a final visit. It was the worst day of my life.

...   .

Six days later, while walking up the aisle, I was in a confused state of mind. Our church believed suicide victims went to the devil. Was that where Dawn was? The hospital doctor assured me when someone truly wants to die; they take the entire bottle of medicine, not just a few extra pills. After reviewing all the evidence, he believed it to be an accidental overdose.

As I knelt in the prayer area of church I said to myself, *Well, God, it looks like you let the devil eat one!* But as my knees touched the floor, a voice popped into my head and said in a conversational way, *What makes you think so?*

I was so startled that I was dumbfounded. What could this be? Nothing like this had ever happened before! I looked around. I was alone in the prayer area. In an instant, a scripture came into my heart. *I've given the body over to the devil for the destruction of the flesh, so the spirit might be saved in the day of the Lord.* (1 Corinthians 5:5)

I suddenly realized God was telling me Dawn was in fact, with the Lord! In that moment, I was a different person. My life had changed! I could have gotten up and danced! I *knew* my Dawny was with the Lord. I knew! There wasn't any possibility for her to be anyplace else.

My daughter's death had come at a time when I had just begun to question the inconsistencies of my church's teachings. The revelation Dawn's soul resided in heaven, which came directly from God, conflicted with what my pastor declared to the whole congregation soon after.

Our pastor, who liked to walk the aisles while preaching, approached me as I sat in an evening service. He got in my face and screamed at me, "And, your daughter is laying in a sinner's grave!"

All I could do was sit there, mortified, as he continued past, resuming his message without missing a beat.

I didn't feel any animosity or anger, but I *knew* he was wrong. This was another piece that was adding up in my mind of the mistakes, the inaccuracies, the lies, the beliefs that this group held that were not biblical. There was no one I could talk to; we weren't allowed to question the preacher or his teachings. So strong was his hold on the congregation, I couldn't even discuss this with my wife! However, God had been leading me all along.

I believe He caused me to become aware of His actual working in the hearts and lives of individuals; that people didn't have to be associated to a particular religion, especially the one I was in. Dawn's death became the catalyst for deeper study which ultimately caused me to leave the cult the following October.

I wasn't able to convince my wife of my convictions. She decided to stay. But, I had come to believe more deeply in the power of prayer.

I held dear three biblical promises that inspire everlasting hope. *"Always give thanks to God the father for everything, in the name of our Lord Jesus Christ."* Ephesians 5:20

"And we know that in all things God works for the good of those who love him, who have been called according to his purpose." Romans 8:28

"Give thanks in all circumstances, for this is God's will for you in Christ Jesus." 1Thessalonians 5:18

Although my eldest child hadn't, I *had* awoken from a coma. We were both set free.

Curtis Delk Rose
Decatur, Indiana

Reborn

"Would you like to go to chapel with us?"

I was six days into a twenty-seven month term at the satellite camp of the medium security prison in Terre Haute, Indiana. At the time, Oklahoma bomber Timothy McVeigh was on death row in the same Federal Correctional Complex. I had spent that first week weeping and feeling sorry for myself. I'd gone from pillar of the community to being exposed as a gambler whose addictions had turned me into a lying, cheating thief who laundered money. *Why should I go to Chapel?* I thought. *What had God done for me?* In my mind, religion was something designed by man that people used to accomplish their own agendas.

"I've a lot more things to worry about than God!" I responded. I was angry, hurt and plagued with guilt. God had abandoned me to get through life on my own. I surely didn't need Him now. I'd lost everything; my job, my reputation, my wife of 23 years and even my freedom. I couldn't look in the mirror. I no longer liked *me*. Why would God?

Two weeks later, Wayne, a thin, towering man, came by my cell and said, "Really, why don't you go to chapel with us?"

Finally, boredom had changed my mind. What did I have to lose? I could get out of my cell where I wasn't accomplishing anything. And so, I went. It was where I met Brother Paul. A few dozen inmates would meet once a week for group discussions. Later, Paul handed out New Testament books which included Psalms and Proverbs.

I couldn't help but notice how *thin* the pages were. "I'll just use these for rolling cigarettes," I said bluntly.

"As long as you tear out a page to roll a cigarette, if you read the page *first*, I will keep you in cigarette wrapping paper as long as you're here," he said, putting a book in my hand. "I recommend you start in Acts."

At first, I blew off my promise and just smoked the pages in my cell. But after a short time something hit me that told me to keep my word. *You told the guy you'd read the page, so go ahead and do it.*

As I began to read, the words seemed to resonate in my heart. Did God want to reach me after all? Did he send me here to change my life? Acts 2: 44-45 struck a nerve. "*...And all that believed were together, and had all things common; and sold their possessions and goods...*" I suddenly realized we prisoners also had nothing and yet had the same things in common!

Within two short days I decided to go to the Gideon's Bible classes and listen to what they had to say. I was hooked!

One day after church services, Chaplain Scott Bonham, who'd become the most influential person in my life, asked, "Have you ever given your life to Christ?" I'd been involved with altar calls at other churches, but this time it would be a real commitment, something I'd never entirely done before. Soon after, I gave my life to Christ at an altar call. Bonham immediately suggested I get baptized.

In the baptistery, Bonham and I stood in a vat of luke-warm water. As he baptized me in the name of the Father, the Son and the Holy Spirit I was lowered until completely im-mersed. Rising up and out of the water, I felt this really strange sensation. The only way to describe it was feeling as if the Holy Spirit *had come into my body!* Indescribable warmth enveloped me. I recognized it as His Love for *me*. I felt instantly cleansed! For the first time, I felt free of the guilt and shame for all the hurt I'd caused. Psalm 51:10 comes closest to describing the impact of my baptism. *"Create in me a clean heart, O God; and renew a right spirit within me."*

From that point on, everything changed. I immediately realized that going to prison was the best thing that could've happened to me, because it was there I found the Lord *sincerely*. Before prison, I was very active in church, but for the sole purpose of having people see me there. I didn't go for my relationship with God. Church had been a tool. I projected this pretty picture of a family man, someone you could trust. Much like a duck in water, I was calm on top of the water, but underneath I had been paddling like hell. Below the surface, no one saw the gambling, the drinking or the failed relationships. They didn't know about my $250,000 gambling habit or how often the utilities got turned off because I didn't pay the bill. They only knew of my successes in business and that I'd been active in high school and college basketball coaching. My former life had been an act, just like the stand-up comedy routines I'd performed before entering prison. This, however, was real!

I couldn't get enough knowledge. Like a sponge, I wanted to absorb more and more about God. Besides Bible studies, I took online classes at Taylor University which I immersed myself in for the 18 months I had left to serve.

When I left prison, I had no job. I was a convicted felon living in a shabby, two bedroom house with nothing to call my own. My furniture consisted of a lawn chair, an egg crate for an end table and a twin bed in a bedroom. I put out 165 résumés before anyone allowed me in the door. Who wanted to hire a convicted felon? But God guided my path and I finally landed a job at a car dealership selling cars.

From there, I became a business development manager for one of the largest dealerships in Indiana. During this time, I got involved with Gideon's and the prison ministry offering hope in Jesus Christ, if they'd allow themselves to receive it. I knew from experience dealing with guilt is like having a millstone around your neck. I wanted to offer the comfort and peace only the Lord can provide. Along the way, I met several chaplains and ministers who asked if I'd do presentations at their churches, which I did. During this time, I also started several gamblers' anonymous support groups in Northeast Indiana. I had become *involved*.

So, when the director of the Pulse Opera House came to watch my performance at the Fort Wayne Civic Theater, then later asked whether I'd consider being a pastor for her church in Warren, Indiana; I turned her down. The last thing I wanted was the confinement of being a pastor. Yes, I wanted to reach as many people as I could and tell them my story; that there's hope in the Lord Jesus. Yes, I'd filled in for a pastor once before. But my life was full, thank you very much. I'd resumed my stand-up comedy routines with my friend, Larry Bower (Morning News Director at WBCL Christian Radio) and had met and married my soul mate, Kim. I was now making nearly a six-figure income as a business development manager. I felt I was doing enough.

I finally gave in to being interviewed and gave a trial sermon at the UCC Church. They were down to 23 parishioners. One week later after interviewing several others, they asked if I'd take the call. Before making a decision, I did my due diligence and looked over their financials. Their numbers had dropped so much; I knew they couldn't afford a full-time pastor. My counter offer was to come in and give the church a dignified death. I could do it on a part-time, temporary basis while continuing my current job. This I would do until the doors closed or we brought enough people in to support a pastor.

They agreed.

I fully expected this to be a temporary assignment. God had other plans! Within six months we had added 49 more souls to our roster and today we've a thriving church, averaging 115 members. We've built a Fellowship Hall with a fully furnished kitchen; the debt paid off within a year. August of 2009 I left my job to become a full-time pastor, taking a tremendous cut in pay. The gambler part of me had resisted this until my wife said, "Is this about money or is this about God?" Her words hit me like a two by four. I became a full-time pastor.

It's truly a love affair at this church, what God's done in my life in crossing the paths of the people in the congregation and this community. I've wrapped myself in Warren or should I say, they've wrapped their arms around me. I do a lot of different functions in the town. And it's all God working through me.

A defining moment of who I had *become,* came with the very first question the call committee had asked in my final interview. "How do you feel about gay people?"

I looked them in the eye and said, "Well, I'm a convicted felon, a compulsive gambler and always will be. I'm divorced. I've robbed, cheated and stole. I'm probably the lowest person you'd ever want to have as a pastor. Don't you have some other questions for me other than how I feel about gay people?"

Being a pastor with a past is who I am. I've learned that no matter how far you've fallen, God's love can and will restore you. I base my ministry on *nobody cares about how much you know, until they know how much you care.* After all, that's what the Lord did for me.

The Rest of the Story...

Until recently, my story would've ended here. However, I've since had a second encounter with the Holy Spirit, the first being my baptism. One June 25, 2014, I'd developed a fever and was taken to Lutheran hospital in Fort Wayne. I had a temperature of 105.5 and was immediately placed in ICU. My team of doctors discovered a blood disease which had gone septic. By Friday evening, the 27th, I was in an induced coma, attached to a ventilator. The doctors told my wife, Kim, they had done all they could. They estimated I had two hours to live.

My church had planned on holding a prayer vigil on Sunday, but the church secretary, Sarah, called everyone and said if they were going to have a prayer vigil, they need to do it *right now!*

Everyone gathered that night. Not only parishioners, but many townspeople I'd come to know through my involvements in Warren. And how did I know that? Because my spirit was there!

I have no memory of how I got there and felt confused at what I was observing. I seemed suspended in the choir loft, looking down at the scene before me. Was I seeing my funeral? As there was no casket, I soon believed otherwise. I saw Reverend Ed Clark, a retired Methodist who'd been filling in for me leading the prayer vigil. He spoke of my healing, not my passing. I then saw him place oil on the foreheads of four deacons, praying with each of them. Later that night, they came to my hospital bed and laid hands on me, praying over me. But I didn't learn of that until later. I continued watching the prayer vigil, feeling waves of love wash over me as they prayed and sang songs.

A good friend and congregant, Jeff Souder, stood and asked if they could sing something upbeat because he thought that's what I'd want. He suggested *How Great Thou Art*. As the song filled the sanctuary, I felt overwhelming gratitude they hadn't given up on me. Afterward, I watched everyone weeping as they left the sanctuary. I felt so loved!

My next memory is the same night at the Salamonie Festival Parade in Warren. I found myself among the crowd lining the sidewalks as if I were standing beside them. I could see many floats passing by with signs that said *Pray for Pastor Scott*. A similar banner lined the sidewalk beside our church. As the floats with banners passed by, I heard cheers from the crowd.

"He's done a lot at the Pulse Theatre and used to emcee the Parade," commented one elderly person.

"He's going to be missed," said another.

Though their words saddened me, I felt such over-whelming love. It was humbling. I didn't deserve this! It was the closest I had ever felt to being called to my heavenly home. Not since Larry Bower had made the three hour trip after my baptism to tell me he'd forgiven me, had I felt so emotional.

When Reverend Clark visited me in the hospital the next day, I was able to describe everything that happened at the prayer vigil. As he confirmed everything I said, I realized I had really been there! Why had I been spared? I believe God had more for me to do or else I'd be dead. I was released from the hospital July 6th and within two to three months got back on my feet. Though I'm not yet at a hundred percent, I'm grateful to be alive.

When I reflect on my spiritual experiences, three scriptures are especially meaningful.

"I know a man in Christ who fourteen years ago was caught up to the third heaven. Whether it was in the body or

out of the body I do not know—God knows. And, I know that this man—whether in the body or apart from body I do not know, but God knows—was caught up to paradise. He heard inexpressible things, things that man is not permitted to tell."
2 Corinthians 12: 2-4

"God is spirit, and his worshipers must worship in spirit and in truth." John 4: 24

"Do you not know that your body is a temple of the Holy Spirit, who is in you, whom you have received from God? You are not your own; you were bought at a price. Therefore honor God with your body." 1 Corinthians 6: 19-20

I'm blessed beyond measure to be able to tell others what Christ did in my life, and I get to experience it over and over again in hopes it will help one person grab that same hope. I was the sinner of sinners, the low of lows. At the height of my gambling, I lied, I cheated, I stole, I womanized. Even today, I do a lot of addiction counseling. I can relate to their weaknesses because I did it all.

The best experience I ever had was that process of humiliation to prison, to letting Christ into my life, to being forgiven by grace and finally to helping others. No one is perfect, not even those in the pulpit. For those broken because of their own fractured religious experiences I say this: *"What man can ruin in the name of religion, God brings back together in the name of Spirituality."*

The small, brown New Testament given to me by Gideon's still sits in my pulpit. Pages 227 through 236 are torn out of it. On page 238, you'll find Acts 4: 12. "Neither is there salvation in any other: for there is none other name under heaven given among men, whereby we must be saved."

I am a testament that Jesus can save the worst of sinners. I've been redeemed. By the power of Christ's love, I have been *reborn*.

Reverend Scott E. Nedberg
Pastor at United Church of Christ
Warren, Indiana

Grace

It was 2 a.m. on a cold December morning. I was suddenly awakened by a dreadful pounding on my door.

"Where *is* she?" I heard a loud voice scream. "Where's Cheyenne? Who's she with?"

I immediately jumped out of bed.

"It's Bill!" my roommate called up the stairwell, recognizing the man through a window.

"Don't let him in!" I yelled, running down the stairs. The man I'd been dating, who'd stayed the night, was right behind me.

Too late! Connie had opened the door and Bill stormed inside. "I'm going to kill you! I'm going to kill you *all*!"

I stood at the bottom of the stairs, terrified and trembling. I knew I was in trouble. I'd made the terrible mistake of seeing another man. A man *other* than Bill.

"I'm going to get my gun and kill you all!" Bill screamed, arms flailing. He looked right at me, pointing his finger. "*You*! Come here!"

All at once I heard a loud buzzing in my ears. It seemed as if I was watching myself from somewhere behind as I took a step toward the infuriated Bill.

Only one thought tumbled from the pandemonium of my mind. *I'm going to die!*

···   ···   ···

I'd been married only a year to my second husband Carlos, and it had been rocky from the start. The day after we wed, he claimed he'd made a mistake. Three months later, unsure of what he wanted; Carlos moved out.

I'd felt abandoned, hurt and confused. My two young sons from a previous marriage needed stability, and in my mind creating a new family was the only way to provide it. Still, I'd ignored the warning signs of yet another poor choice in men. At first, Carlos had been sweet and considerate. But within weeks of getting married, a secretive, argumentative side of him emerged, culminating in a blow up when I awoke early one morning to find a duffle bag by the entrance. As a recruiter in the Army, he'd leave for work in his uniform. So, finding a bag near the door didn't make sense.

"What the heck is this?" I asked, viewing the duffle bag. Peering inside, I could see civilian clothes, deodorant and aftershave.

"Oh that," Carlos said, grabbing it. "It's nothing."

"What do you mean *nothing*? What do you need it for?"

"I sometimes go out for beer after work," he said, frowning.

"And, you can't wear your uniform?"

"Leave me alone," he said, turning away. "I'm only having a couple beers."

It wasn't long after that Carlos had left us. However, within weeks, he'd again changed his mind. With persistent phone calls, he convinced me he wanted our marriage to work. Promising he'd stop going to bars, he moved back in shortly before being deployed to Korea.

With this turn of events, I once again hoped for the best. I'd blamed his erratic behavior on the recent death of his mother and convinced myself it wasn't *me* he was unhappy with. He was simply upset with life. Time, I believed, would make everything right.

And so it was with eager anticipation I awaited his mid-term visit home that July. But, what I'd hoped would be a joyous reunion, evolved into a month of arguing, name calling and heated words. Where had this ugly side of Carlos come from? He'd scream and yell at the slightest thing. It was almost as if he were trying to goad me into fights for no apparent reason. I couldn't understand. What had I done? What had happened to cause this change in him?

After his exhausting visit, Carlos returned to Korea that August. I couldn't stop thinking about all that had transpired in one short year. My gut was telling me he was up to something. I played over and over in my mind the argument about the duffle bag. Unable to let it go, I had badgered him for weeks until he had finally admitted he'd been going to *strip bars*. That's why he needed his civilian clothes. I thought about the arguments, the defensiveness and his change in behavior.

All at once it struck me like a thunderbolt. He's cheating! That *has* to be it! How could I have been so stupid? My world had suddenly collapsed. Everything I'd worked and hoped for had broken into a million pieces, shattered and scattered beneath my feet. At that moment, I felt I had no future and no hope of putting it together again.

As I recalled the lies, the demeaning words and deceptive behavior, I became furious! How could he do this after everything I'd done to make our marriage work? My heart rebelled at his callousness, which brought my own ugly side to the fore. *I'll show him! I'll get even! He'll soon learn what it feels like to be cheated on, lied to and abandoned!*

And so without telling Carlos, I moved to Fort Wayne, Indiana where I found a rental for me, my two kids and a roommate, Connie. I made good on my threat, finding not only one man to be with, but two. Deep within me, a gentle voice prodded, *You shouldn't be doing this.* Yet, I didn't stop. Carlos had hurt me and I wanted to hurt him back. It never occurred to me there'd be repercussions for my retaliation. I'd become consumed with revenge. And for a while, it tasted sweet.

Then, in a split second, it all changed...

I stood trembling in front of an infuriated ex-lover while my boys huddled on the steps, crying. Bill pointed his finger at me.

"You! Come here!"

I heard a loud buzzing in my ears as I seemed to watch myself go toward him.

All at once, the man I'd been sharing my bed with, pushed me aside. Calvin stepped forward, wordlessly advancing toward Bill. In an explosion of violence, Bill had him pinned to the floor, beating him with his fists and anything else within reach. For five long minutes, the beating continued. Calvin didn't utter a sound. He lay curled in a ball and covering his head, took the pummeling.

Finally, with one final threat, Bill ran out the front door. We immediately called the police, filing a report before taking Calvin to the hospital. Thankfully, his injuries weren't life threatening and he soon left the emergency room.

But I felt devastated. Thinking about what had happened; I wondered about how it had gotten to this point. Before, I'd done things to get back at others who'd hurt me and I never once considered it my fault. I realized this *was* my fault and I'd caused this by the choices and decisions I'd made. Nobody else was to blame.

I decided I'd never try to get revenge on anybody again, because I hadn't hurt Carlos at all. What I tried to do to him, I did to myself. I'd put my family in this situation for no reason than my own selfish desires.

Filled with remorse, I tried praying. I desperately wanted to be forgiven for everything I'd done. As I recalled the terrible beating Calvin took in my place, God opened the eyes of my heart. *That is what I did for you on the cross. I took the punishment even though you were guilty and deserved it.*

I suddenly felt awful, broken and humiliated at the same time grateful and astounded beyond comprehension how God had done that for me! It was a huge revelation. The floodgates of feeling unloved had burst open and begun draining away.

From my earliest memories, I hadn't felt loved, especially by my earthly father. It seemed to repeat itself with each relationship I made. Not knowing what real love felt like, I found men who mirrored my dad; cold and distant. Even though I often chose unwisely, God wanted me to know that *He* loved me. He loved me enough to grab me by the collar and say, *You need to stop making the choices you're making because if you don't, you're going to end up dead.*

I believed Him!

I immediately packed my bags and moved back home. My relationship with my husband eventually failed, but my relationship with God flourished. Even to this day, I'm amazed how God had kept us alive in that volatile situation.

Since then, I've found two scriptures that have sustained and reaffirmed God's love toward me. Reading them, I felt God was speaking directly to me and my brokenness.

"Fear not; for thou shalt not be ashamed; neither be thou confounded; for thou shalt not be put to shame; for thou shalt forget the shame of thy youth, and shalt not remember the reproach of thy widowhood any more.

For thy Maker is thine husband; the Lord of hosts is His name; and thy Redeemer the Holy One of Israel; The God of the whole earth shall He be called.

For the Lord hath called thee as a woman forsaken and grieved in spirit, and a wife of youth, when thou wast refused,"saith thy God.

"For a small moment have I forsaken thee; but with great mercies will I gather thee.

In a little wrath I hid My face from thee for a moment; but with everlasting kindness will I have mercy on thee,' saith the Lord thy Redeemer.

"For this is as the waters of Noah unto Me: for as I have sworn that the waters of Noah should no more go over the earth; so have I sworn that I would not be wroth with thee, nor rebuke thee.

For the mountains shall depart, and the hills be removed; but My kindness shall not depart from thee, neither shall the covenant of My peace be removed," saith the Lord that hath mercy on thee.

"O thou afflicted, tossed with tempest, and not comforted, behold, I will lay thy stones with fair colours, and lay thy foundations with sapphires. And I will make thy windows of agates, and thy gates of carbuncles, and all thy borders of pleasant stones.

And all thy children shall be taught of the Lord; and great shall be the peace of thy children. In righteousness shalt thou be established; thou shalt be far from oppression; for thou shalt not fear; and from terror; for it shall not come near thee.

Behold, they shall surely gather together, but not by Me; whosoever shall gather together against thee shall fall for thy sake.

Behold, I have created the smith that bloweth the coals in the fire, and that bringeth forth an instrument for his work; and I have created the waster to destroy. No weapon that is formed against thee shall prosper; and every tongue that shall rise against thee in judgment thou shalt condemn. This is the heritage of the servants of the Lord, and their righteousness is of Me," saith the Lord. Isaiah, 54: 4-17 (KJV)

"But he himself went on a day's journey into the wilderness, and came and sat down under a juniper tree; and he requested for himself that he might die; and said, "It is enough; now O Lord, take away my life; for I am not better than my fathers."

And as he lay and slept under a juniper tree, behold, then an Angel touched him, and said unto him, "Arise and eat."

And he looked, and, behold there was a cake baken on the coals, and a cruse of water at his head. And he did eat and drink, and laid him down again. And, the Angel of the Lord came again the second time, and touched him, and said, "Arise and eat; because the journey is too great for thee." 1Kings 19: 4-7. (KJV)

Though my life hasn't been smooth sailing, I've discovered that God's always with me, making beauty out of the ashes of my life. I'm learning to trust Him as He leads me where He wants me to be. And through it all, I hold onto grace given from the cross when my Lord died for *me*. It's just as real as on that cold December morning when another took my place.

Cheyenne, B.
Chicago, Illinois

Spiritual Warfare

"For our struggle is not against flesh and blood, but against the rulers, against the authorities, against the powers of this dark world and against the spiritual forces of evil in the heavenly realms." Ephesians 6:12

Something had awakened me. I listened, suddenly alert. There it was again! Tapping sounds above my bed, as if coming from the attic. Not only taps above me, but I could now hear tapping noises all over the house. It was as if a light bulb had suddenly gone off in my head. With clarity that I'd been denying for weeks, I suddenly knew...

...   .

Ever since we'd moved into the home we'd rented, strange things had occurred. First were the three loud knocks at my front door around two a.m. No one had been there. I'd dismissed it as someone knocking at the wrong house before realizing their mistake. The same thing happened two days later. Confused, a dim panic began growing within me. This was a new experience. I didn't understand what was going on. I felt scared, but of what?

Next, my fourteen year old daughter, Kaelyne, began having nightmares and refused sleeping in her room. She would dream of being chased by something evil; vampire-like. In her dreams she saw tribal diamond shaped patterns on her bedroom walls in colors of red-green and brown-yellow. Once, she dreamt of a human-shaped mass standing in her room. She always awakened panicked and frightened. Another time she awoke, terrorized at seeing a black mass forming into some sort of animal crouching on her chest. She now slept in my bed.

Then tapping, knocking and strange sounds began emanating from the attic. Most of the activity took place between two and three in the morning. I tried dismissing them as noises a house makes when settling. But, as I now lay in bed, the fear I'd tried holding at bay finally took over. The knocks at the door, the nightmares my daughter had been experiencing and the loud tapping noises above the ceiling all pointed to one thing. Something evil was occurring in this house!

All at once, my daughter awoke beside me. She too, heard the constant rapping throughout the house. Terrified, we jumped out of bed and awakened my twelve-year old son to flee the house, spending the night on a friends' couch.

About this time, Kyra, a longtime friend, had agreed to stay with us. She brought along her dog, Gizmo, which upon entering the house, immediately urinated on the floor. After cleaning it up, we all watched TV before retiring. Both Kyra and Gizmo slept at the foot of my bed on a mattress. Gizmo remained uneasy and growled often throughout the night. The next morning, Kyra told me she'd had a nightmare in which she saw herself trying to crawl from the floor to my bed, but some force held her back. This was just one more thing to ponder over, another element to digest. Whatever this *thing* was, it had the capability to affect anyone who entered my home.

I soon called a local church, describing to the reception-ist the tapping noises, my daughter's dreams and that something just wasn't right. She assured me someone would return my call.

They didn't.

I called a second church and left a voice message that something strange was happening in my home and to *please call me*. Nobody returned my call. The third church I called went straight to voicemail. I hung up without leaving a message.

I even attended a Sunday church service where they had an altar call for those who needed prayer. I went forward, breaking down in tears as I described what was happening in my home.

"Oh, it is that bad?" a woman said, making a sypathetic expression. We prayed together for the Lord's protection. She then said she'd have her prayer group pray for my family. However, she didn't offer any direction in what I should do or whether I could even talk to their priest or anyone, for that matter.

Did they all think this was a joke? Did they believe me mentally ill? I felt helpless. I didn't know what else to do.

Things then began happening with increasing intensity. However, the worst was yet to come. The knocks and taps were now joined by new, disturbing sounds of something being dragged in the kitchen as well as the attic above. Eerily, the bathroom faucet once turned itself on. I started to find bruises shaped like bite marks on my body. I had no idea how I'd received them.

Two days later, I contacted the Puget Sound Ghost Hunters. I'd never imagined I'd be driven to research the internet for this type of service. Their first investigation came within ten days of my call and exactly one month after moving in.

The investigative team recorded tapping noises, moaning, growling sounds and voices that spoke profanity. Two days later, while changing my bed sheets, I found claw marks on my foam mattress! This shook me to my core for the sheets were not torn. I'd been unaware this *thing* had been beside my bed as I'd slept. What was it trying to do to me?

The activity grew more sinister during subsequent investigations which included scratches and more bite marks on both myself and investigators. Also recorded were loud footsteps running across the ceiling as well as whistle-like sounds and poundings noises.

The next two investigations included many attempts to get the spirits to depart. Both Donna and Ken exclaimed out-loud, *"This wasn't their home and they needed to leave!"* The team members had grown sterner with their rebukes when their research revealed this wasn't a typical haunting. Yet the phenomena continued.

In an attempt to get rid of the entity, Donna, co-owner of PSGH, recommended we try something else called Reiki. (Reiki is a healing technique based on the principle that the therapist can channel energy into the patient by means of touch, to activate the natural healing processes of the patient's body and restore physical and emotional well-being.)

They brought in Stephanie, a Reiki Master, who performed movements over our bodies without touching us. As she worked, bruises began forming on her arms out of thin air. We used a prayer circle to dispel our home of negativity, ending with a house blessing using sage and more prayers.

Afterward, Stephanie assured us, "The house was well."

The *house*, however, was not amused.

The next few days, new and disturbing activities arose. Booming noises that were difficult to describe began happening throughout the house. Even the TV in my bedroom, which

I used to drown out noises, began to emit its own creaking, tapping sounds. Once, I'd awakened from sleep around 4 a.m. to see vivid, brown-yellow diamond patterns covering my bedroom walls. They looked just like what Kaelyne had described. After blinking for several seconds, they gradually disappeared and the walls once again became white.

I realized it wasn't over. Nothing had worked; not investigations, not house anointing, sage blessings or even Reiki had gotten rid of whatever was haunting my home. It felt like I lived in a war-zone. With a heavy heart, I contacted Puget Sound Ghost Hunters again.

After their fourth and last investigation, I'd awakened after midnight sensing something over me. Once my eyes adjusted to the dim light of the alarm clock, I saw a black mass hovering above me. My daughter had half-awakened to my movements and immediately said, "What *is* that?"

"What?" I replied. I still didn't believe what I was seeing.

"That, over there," she said, looking in its direction. She then rolled over and fell back asleep. Thankfully, she didn't remember seeing it the next day.

This was another, more sinister incident. I'd been getting used to the tapping, strange noises and bruises, but how far could this go? It felt like a scene from a movie but it was actually happening in my own home. Could this black mass swallow someone? Would they disappear?

The very next morning as I readied for work, a horribly foul odor permeated the bathroom, burning my eyes. A combination of rotting fish, eggs and feces couldn't adequately describe the stench. I nearly vomited as I ran from the room.

That's when I recalled my daughter speaking to a copse of pine trees across the street, behind our neighbor's house. "Hi, whatever you are," she had said as we'd driven up our driveway. This was the place where Stephanie had claimed the bad energy she had removed from the house, had gone. I now wondered if my daughter's words could've invited them back in?

Throughout this time, my friend, Kyra, often stayed with us or we went to her home when we were too frightened to stay. This was in spite of the fact something had followed Kyra home after her first night at my house. Once, a heavy kitchen appliance had flown out of her cupboard and landed across the room. She'd also experienced a black mass hovering behind her as she looked in her bathroom mirror.

I thanked God this didn't sever our friendship. Kyra was a strong woman. She never blinked an eye or tried explaining away these events. She opened her home to me and the kids numerous times, even leaving the comfort of her bed to sleep on my floor. Her attitude bespoke of her determination to help me figure this out and see it to the end.

Though I tried remaining strong for my children, I felt emotionally exhausted. I'd long since stopped using the excuse the noises were from a settling house. The kids often expressed their fear and dislike of the house. They begged to go and live with their dad in California. I knew that was impossible. Even if he wanted to, he wasn't in a position to take them. I could only tell them over and over God was their protector. But, *would* He protect us? *Could* He?

Each day seemed to bring another incident. It was 1:30 a.m. I was trying to fall asleep, which was difficult considering I kept the lights on and TV blaring. I suddenly heard what sounded like a string of firecrackers set off in the attic. Fast and loud, they seemed to be popping above the wall that separates kitchen from living room. Then, about forty minutes later they began again, only closer. Now, the racket sounded above the wall that separated *my room* from the living room. Frightened at this new aberration, I jumped out of bed. But where could I go? I went to my daughter's room to escape. The taps taunted me by knocking directly above my head as I lay next to my daughter, and then traveled down the long hallway to the other side of the house. There was no escape.

I got back into my own bed knowing I wouldn't sleep that night. I had hardly slept for a long time. I felt absolutely lost, frightened and in total despair. Everything I had tried, failed. A personal friend had anointed my home with oil; PSGH attempted many times to cleanse the home as did Stephanie, the Reiki Master.

Even friends, whom I'd turned to, discouraged my trusting in a higher power. "It's nice you're into God, but don't go overboard like some do in their faith," said one.

"Tone it down," said another when I spoke of my relationship with Jesus. Regardless of their words, prayer was my last vestige of hope.

I recalled a dream I'd had about a year ago. *I'd dreamt I was on an old ship at night, pitch black, hurricane winds and sea wild with waves as tall as mountains. Flashes of lightening revealed the ships' appearance to be similar to a vessel from the days of Christopher Columbus. I was standing beside rails of a ship. Suddenly, someone stood next to me. Though I couldn't see through the darkness, I instantly knew it to be my Father. Not my earthly father, but my heavenly Father. He said, "Jump with me into this raging black sea." I trusted Him and together we jumped. In my dream I woke up on a beautiful sunny beach. We both lay face down in the sand. As I lifted my head and opened my eyes, I looked at who held my hand while I lay on a beautiful, sunny, tropical beach. It was Jesus!*

I wouldn't give up on my Lord. I may not understand what was happening or why, but I refused to believe God had abandoned me.

The next day, I hung a crucifix on the wall. I distinctly heard growling while doing so. However, I ignored the menacing noise. I told myself *that just didn't happen.* It was my way of coping. I was near the breaking point.

My stress hit their highest levels by the next night. My children, who never argued, had been continuously fighting. In a fit of rage, my son had thrown a dinner plate before storming outside. Instead of breaking, the dish embedded itself in the wall! Perfectly level, it would've held food without it slipping off. Kaelyne and I looked at each other in total disbelief before I walked over and dislodged the plate. *What had just happened?* I feared each new occurrence. I feared even more the phenomena would continue to worsen.

Soon after, Kaelyne had come into my room around midnight saying she saw something near her bedroom door. Later that night, my cell phone flew off the table.

Though I didn't attend church regularly, I prayed and believed in God. I had a personal relationship with Jesus. *Why was this happening to me?* I now felt lost, frightened and in total despair. I could no longer sleep. If I did, it was only with lights and TV blaring or after the sun came up. My friends said I looked lost and exhausted. I often felt sheer terror.

Worst of all, I couldn't move away. I'd borrowed $2,000 to move into this house and had yet to pay back a penny. I couldn't ask for more.

In May, I received an email from Ken, co-owner of the Puget Sound Ghost Hunters. I could scarcely digest his next words. "*We've spoken to others in our industry and now believe you have the beginnings of a demon infestation. This goes beyond our services. We feel it's time to put you in con-*

tact with a man who's experienced similar events in his life and has overcome them. He's a Demonologist. His name is Bill Vaile."

I contacted him immediately.

Right away, Bill stated God was the answer to this situation. What I had been doing wasn't enough. He helped me understand the behavior of demons, suggesting I read about demonology and angels. "Fighting this is a journey, not a single battle. There'll be days you'll feel exhausted and want to give up. You mustn't! These entities will try wearing you down. The devil's a bully whose strength lies in our weakness and his weakness is our strength, which is a belief in God. We shouldn't fear, but worship God because evil can't exist in a house of God."

Bill stressed the importance of my growing in faith because this was my battle to fight. "Please realize a minister or priest or even myself, are only antibodies that weaken a disease or supports your immune system so your body can do the actual fighting. We can help, but you must finish the job."

I felt so thankful I could share what was happening with someone who'd had similar experiences. Anticipation surged through me. *I wanted to learn everything*. With Bill's knowledge, I'd surely conquer this evil.

Besides reading my Bible, I began to read everything I could get my hands on about the enemy living in my house. I began praying out loud and stating in a firm voice, "This house belongs to Jesus. Leave in the name of Jesus."

I also learned about tricks the enemy used. "If you heard me tapping at 4:30 in the morning," Bill once said, "would it frighten you? Is it the taps that scare you or the unknown? Just ignore the taps or say, 'I no longer fear you and my faith in Christ is growing stronger through *your* presence, so go away!' "

However, it wasn't until I recited a prayer that Bill wrote himself, that I felt I'd hit the entity's "spiritual nerve."

Late one afternoon, I held a paper in front of me and read in a loud voice. *"In the name of Jesus Christ you are commanded to leave this place and never bother me or my family again, here or anywhere we might choose to venture, now or anytime in the future! Jesus Christ is my Savior and my protector and in His protection we no longer fear you! We are saved by Him, are protected by Him and by His word, by His protection, through His salvation and in His name we order you to leave us alone. In the name of Jesus Christ you are commanded to leave this place now! You are not invited here, are no longer welcome here and any contracts with you in the past are hereby cancelled and revoked by Him and by us in His name and for His glory! We have been washed in His blood and absolved of all sin so you have no control and no contract over us any longer! We are in His hands and in His protection now and in His name I ask that angels be sent to watch over us, protect us, and to make sure you leave now and never return under threat of being bound to your own worst fears! In the name of Jesus Christ you are commanded to leave this place and never bother me or my family again! Amen."*

All at once the ceiling went crazy! What sounded like strings of firecrackers began exploding above every room in the house. Never had activity occurred this early in the day before. Fearing what might happen, I called a friend who was at that moment, deep in prayer.

She came immediately, bringing her Bible. We prayed first and then she began reading out of the Bible. As she did, the ceiling launched its firecracker activity once again, but with less intensity. She looked at the ceiling, surprised.

"Ohhh!" she said, before dropping her eyes to continue reading.

That was the beginning of the end.

Dislodging the entities ended up being a two-month process. And true to Bill's word, there were days I felt emotionally exhausted and drained. However, the spiritual weapons in my arsenal proved to be more powerful. With renewed confidence I prayed multiple times a day, using Christ's ultimate authority. As I grew stronger in faith, it became less a terror and more an adversary I could conquer with the help of God.

I felt I received just that assurance, late one night. I awoke to a sense of something around me. I saw what looked like a huge force, silver and shiny emanating from a wall from floor to ceiling. I heard a subtle noise in my head, like a plane landing on the roof. This force was bright with silver, and humming. And although I said, "Protect us Jesus," four times, it did not feel evil. All at once, it was gone.

Gone too, were the entities in my home.

Later, I took a demonology course taught by a Catholic priest to help me understand what had happened in my home. I learned how prayer rebukes evil spirits and how denial is their greatest ally. When one shines the light of truth on evil, it becomes our greatest weapon.

I also shared my new-found wisdom with Kyra, who used Bill's approach to rid her home of her own frightening visitations.

Before this happened, I'd had a casual relationship with God. I believed He was my protector, but I never knew *how* to seek His help. I didn't understand about different spirits and that I could rebuke those spirits in the name of Jesus Christ. Nor did I grasp the full power of God; I could ask the Lord of Hosts to send his angels to protect my family. I now realize He allows trials for our own good. He allows us to bear specific crosses because it leads us to Heaven. I'm thankful this ordeal only lasted five months, from the time we moved in until God drove it out.

Though I've yet to sleep with my bedroom door closed, I no longer fear evil like I did. If I ever feel uneasy, the feelings simply induce extra prayer time with my Lord.

Most importantly, I've come to appreciate the power of God, the Holy Spirit and Jesus!

And, that appreciation came through a man named Bill Vaile. I owe my existence and sanity to him. He says otherwise. He'll say he only guided me. But he really gave me life through a reintroduction to the saving grace of Jesus. He provided me a path to a deeper relationship with Christ than I ever had. I owe Bill everything.

In my many searches through the Bible, I've come to draw great comfort in its words. Not in the least from Psalm 23, especially the 4th verse, *"yea, though I walk through the valley of the shadow of death, I will fear no evil; for you are with me; your rod and your staff, they comfort me."*

Also, *"Do not be afraid of sudden terror, nor of trouble from the wicked when it comes; for the Lord will be your con-fidence, and will keep your foot from being caught."* Proverbs 3: 25-26

These remind me the power of the Lord is greater than the powers of darkness. Through those dark times, I drew closer to God and His Word. Previously, I'd been caught up with world views, money, gossiping and envy. None of them mean anything to me now. Since those events, I read the Bible regularly and practice spiritual warfare daily. And, I thank God for Bill Vaile.

Michele Hernaez
Lakewood, Washington

Unfailing Love

"Lord, what do you want from me?" I asked from the depths of my soul. "There's got to be more! I can't keep living day in and day out with this place of emptiness." No one was at home as I stood that afternoon in my living room. I felt angry. I had been searching for fulfillment, searching for a closer relationship with God. I then lay on the floor face down, my self-will broken as I outstretched my arms like a cross. I began to cry. "I know you're doing something in me, but I need to know what it is, *you want?*"

...   .

Though I'd grown up in church, it left me feeling empty. I wanted, needed something more. I knew there had to be more to living than following a set of "religious rules." I didn't know what *it* was; and so there came a time when I just walked away.

I was 21 years old and pregnant with my first child. I worked in intensive care at a large hospital in a job I loved as a registered nurse (RN). It was amazing. I learned a lot and enjoyed the adrenaline rush. I also lived with my boyfriend, Jimmy. But I had experienced a dream so vivid, so surreal; it caused me to reevaluate my life.

In this dream, I was back in my childhood church. All of a sudden, a featureless dark figure had entered and opened fire. Though it appeared to be a .22 rifle, it sprayed bullets like a machine gun. I was hit, falling flat to the ground. I knew others around me had also been struck, for he had aimed at every church member.

I began to feel my spirit lifting from my body. It appeared milky white, yet transparent. I looked down and saw that I had already come halfway out. In a panic, my *spirit* arms grabbed my body to pull my soul back in, screaming, "No! No! I can't go yet! What about Jimmy? What about our unborn baby?"

Even though I was dreaming, I felt every sensation as if it were happening *in the natural.*

Then all at once, I saw this brilliant, white light. It blinded me. It surrounded me. It engulfed me with warmth and peace. But I wasn't ready to go! I had work to do. I wanted a life with Jimmy. I wanted to raise our kids.

And then, I awoke. I found myself under the covers, scrunched in a ball, my eyes tightly closed. One hand covered my eyes as if trying to dim the brightness of the light. After a few seconds I bolted upright, my heart racing and drenched in sweat.

I had no idea what I'd just experienced. I didn't know what it meant. All I knew was I felt terrified, for I felt as if I were dying.

I had so much ahead of me. *What was going on?* And yet, the dream caused me to seek more of God than what I'd been doing. I could no longer simply go through the motions. I couldn't just attend church or read daily devotions without engaging my heart and mind.

And so began my journey of crying out to the Lord.

I became driven to know more about Jesus apart from religion. I began to be open to more of the supernatural and I hungered to learn about it. It was scary and I was still a bit skeptical, but I knew there was something *real* about it.

Jimmy and I started to attend a church in our town, Cross Bridge Community Church. In addition to Sunday services, I also attended a women's Bible study and our family attended a small group. At every turn, God placed people in my path that spoke words of life over me and called out treasures the Lord placed within me that I couldn't see. He provided this at the right time and the right season. They were exactly what I needed.

I developed a relationship with the Lord to the point I could feel His hand leading me in specific directions. As I questioned Him, I would sense His answers. I began to seek "yes" and "no" answers to questions. I had entered into the infant stages of hearing God's voice.

While at Cross Bridge, I went on a mission trip to Costa Rica in July, 2009. We ran a sports camp for the local children and provided a Bible lesson every day. I saw God move during our sports camp. Initially, we planned to host a basketball camp. When we arrived at the camp site, there were no basketball hoops, so we hosted a soccer camp instead. We had to let go of our agenda and follow the Lord. Now, it makes sense. Soccer is what these kids know and play. They didn't play basketball, nor did we know if they liked basketball, but we knew they loved soccer!

The week prior to my trip we moved back to our hometown, Decatur, Indiana. At this time in life, we were married and with two children. I worked part-time as a nurse for an oral surgeon as well as "as needed" at the local hospital on the medical surgical ICU floor.

While living in Decatur, we started attending a church different from my hometown church. Fifteen months after my trip to Costa Rica, Jimmy and I were given the opportunity to travel on a mission trip to Haiti. I worked in the Mission of Hope clinic. I kept busy seating patients, obtaining health histories, taking vitals, performing nursing duties and assisting the physician. Jimmy worked with a construction team, building and painting.

For the first time, I learned what it looked like to integrate ministry with medicine. I had the misconception that I had to do one or the other, medicine or ministry. I'd never been exposed to the integration of two different fields. In Haiti, the Lord began to have me reach out and pray for people.

I may not have understood their language nor they mine, but when I prayed for those who came to the clinic, we both felt God's presence. The warmth and peace of the Holy Spirit would come upon me, my whole body feeling like fire with occasional jolts of electricity. As this happened, patients would start crying, tightly squeezing my hand. And after we prayed, they often hugged me while speaking in Creole. I didn't understand their words but I recognized their gratitude.

Before, I'd felt this emptiness in me. I now realized serving others had become a big part of who I was. I loved talking, listening and spending time with people. I loved being able to use my natural gifts of medicine and have the freedom to integrate it with ministry.

I felt so alive! Something new burned within me. I wanted to go home, sell everything and live the life of a missionary. Jimmy wasn't so convinced. Yet, I felt God whispering; *Where I've placed you, that is your mantle. That is your platform. I'm going to position you in places where you have the freedom to release ministry.*

After returning home and in addition to Sunday services, I started attending house churches*, prayer meetings at various churches, women's Bible studies and conferences hosted by churches other than the church we attended.

My hunger for the Lord grew; but, for what purpose? What was I put on earth to do? It had been five years since my dream. I truly felt God had led me at every step. In each season, at every juncture it was, *OK, now it's time for this.* Or, *now we're going to learn something else.* And then, *Now I'm going to take you here.*

The desire to know what God wanted from me became a burning passion. But I didn't know how to discover it. I didn't know how to find it. My hunger for the deeper parts of the Spirit grew to the point I cried out to Him while home alone.

Initially, I was angry and frustrated because I never received an answer. Grumbling, I cried out, "Lord, what do you want from me? There's got to be more! I can't keep living day in and day out, with this place of emptiness." I'd been searching for fulfillment in my heart, but never found it. As I lay on the floor, my body stilled, my mind cleared and I cried out to the Lord. My feelings of anger and frustration disappeared and my heart felt the Lord's peace as well as His stillness. Relief flooded my mind. "I know you're doing something in me, but I need to know what it is. What do you want with me?"

The Lord said, *You're going to open a clinic.*

I replied, "What do you mean?" All of a sudden, a picture or vision popped into my head. I saw a sign that said *Unfailing Love* and the sign also said *1 John 4:19.*

I jumped up off the floor where I had been laying, "I've got to write this down!" I found a post-it note and wrote what I'd seen. I didn't know the scripture off the top of my head, so I grabbed my Bible and looked it up. It read, *"We love, because He first loved us."*

Something deep inside me felt as if I just received an answer to my emptiness. I felt a birthing, a strong desire within my spirit suddenly ignited. I knew the clinic was my calling.

At last, I received the missing piece of the puzzle. This is what I'm supposed to do! *Wow!* I thought, *That's really good!* And, then moments later I questioned, "How am I going to do this?"

Jesus replied, *Go back to school.*

"Didn't we try this already? It didn't work out too well," I said, recalling I'd taken classes three years ago. However, the timing hadn't been right, and I ended up only taking one summer class before quitting.

Again, Jesus said, *Go back to school. The door is open.*

How could I do that? I thought. *I don't know how this is going to work!* I still owed for my undergrad studies. I was mom to two young children. Here it was March. My third child was due in May and school would start in August. I didn't see how this would fit into my schedule.

I'd been praying for an answer and here I was, immediately questioning it. "Ok, Lord," I said. "I don't know how, but I'll do it." I didn't have all the answers or resources lined up, but I surrendered my flesh to Jesus and said, "Have your way. Teach me to trust you and to walk by faith, not by sight."

I then stuck that post-it note on the refrigerator to remind me of my goal.

I didn't realize until later, that faith is an *action* word. It simply means to walk *with Him*. The Lord can give visions and direction to lead us, but it requires that we move our feet.

And move I did.

Two weeks later, I applied to the University of St. Francis to obtain a Master of Science in Nursing. After my interview, I got right in. "All right, Lord, if you're going to have me do this, you've got to help me pay for it." His immediate response came in the form of me receiving a grant for half my tuition being paid every year!

God wasn't done with surprises, however. My third year, we students were informed St. Francis had received a large grant and money would be dispersed according to how they judged essays on what we planned on doing after school. I wrote about Unfailing Love Clinic.

I ended up receiving all of my tuition being paid my last year of school. The Lord had answered another prayer. I graduated owing only one-third the cost of acquiring a master's degree. Starting the journey of returning to school I didn't know I'd get the scholarship to pay for half my tuition. I didn't know my whole last year would be paid for with a grant. I stepped out in faith and God showed up and blessed me.

Of course, there were many ups and downs. I learned what it looks like to be in relationship with the Lord. I had moments of doubt and unbelief *in the natural* whether I could actually do this. I'd look at my load and assignments and feel overwhelmed. There were times I'd cry out to him, "Lord, you picked the wrong person! I can't do this!" Yet without fail, the Lord would always show me the way.

If not for His tender mercies, I would've failed. Through grace, God had been cultivating our relationship every step of the way. With every encounter, with every blessing I drew closer to His heart. My prayers began to change. I now often prayed, "Lord, I want to see through your eyes. I want your heart. I want my mind to be set on things above and not of this life." It helped me to slow down and know how important it is *to be still in the Lord.*

My time searching, praying and crying out to Jesus helped me become stronger. It created a deeper yearning, a more powerful desire to seek God's presence. It started out small, but the act of seeking Him increased my desire to know Him more. It caused me to hunger more for Him and the things of eternity verses of the things of life. And, that's when

He began to forge a well so deep within me that His love would never run dry.

As I spent time with the Lord, He began to answer back. At first, it seemed more of a feeling, an intuition of what He wanted from me. Gradually, His voice became clearer. It reminded me of when God told the prophet Elijah to go stand on the mountain, for the Lord was about to pass by. *"Then a great and powerful wind tore the mountain apart and shattered the rocks before the Lord, but the Lord was not in the wind. After the wind there was an earthquake, but the Lord was not in the earthquake. After the earthquake came a fire, but the Lord was not in the fire. And after the fire came a gentle whisper. When Elijah heard it, he pulled his cloak over his face and went out and stood at the mouth of the cave." 1Kings, 19: 11-13*

As I grew closer to the Lord, spoke to Him, prayed for guidance; He responded as my mentor and friend. If I became too tired to study, He'd tell me to go to bed. If I presented Him with seemingly insurmountable problems, He'd remove those obstacles from my path. I had to learn to lose control and let go of my own ways and agenda. As my love for the Lord grew, so did my desire to learn more of who He is and what He has in store for me. I know I'll never understand fully the bigness and greatness of God. But what I do know is this; He's in pursuit of everybody. He desires for our hearts to cry out for Him.

Then, my final year in school, the Lord began leading me to do things that didn't make sense.

Make a proposal.

A proposal? I didn't even know what a proposal was! However, I had become involved with a friends' ministry where people of various professions prayed for people at Lutheran Hospital in Fort Wayne. The leader of this ministry, a female pastor and I became friends. We spent a lot of time together in prayer.

I'd been helping the pastor on her leadership team and I assisted with building the foundation of the ministry. During this time we created a strategic plan. I used the fundamentals I learned to help create a proposal and case for the clinic. I sat with the Lord and He told me to create a mission and vision statement. He then led me to create titles of the table of contents, even giving me the idea to use Roman numerals. I began to research and fill in the rest. With it, I outlined the Heart and Vision of Unfailing Love Clinic. This included our beliefs,** vision statement,*** as well as our goals, present**** and future.*****

As part of the proposal and under subdivision: *The Vision of Unfailing Love*, I wrote an overview.

> "Unfailing Love is a non-profit, free medical clinic available to individuals who are uninsured or underinsured and living less than 200% of the poverty level. The Heart of Unfailing Love is to rise up the local community to volunteer and serve others, first locally, then reaching out past the borders of the county and expanding worldwide. The clinic will focus on health promotion and illness prevention by providing free healthcare, education, and preventative screenings. Although it is free, it is not a crutch for individuals to use because it is free. It is a resource to provide and meet immediate needs while promoting individual independence."

Mission Statement.

"Unfailing Love is a non-profit medical clinic that provides resources and services to promote health and healing of one's body, mind and spirit."

Vision Statement.

"Uniting a community as one body under the head of Christ to reach out and serve the Nations."

I kept it for two months. I remember thinking, "I researched and typed this proposal and printed it out. Now, what do you want me to do with it?" A few months later God gave me the answer.

I want you to start reaching out to a board.

"Okay!" I thought. I could see things were starting to move.

Take your proposal.

By then, I'd learned to not doubt the Lords' promptings. I thought of positions necessary to help establish the clinic. If I held the position of President, I'd need a Vice President, Treasurer, Secretary and someone else from the medical field. With God's help I chose four individuals who loved Jesus, could walk by faith and who believed in the mission and vision of Unfailing Love Clinic. They weren't business men or women, but they had a heart for God's people.

I called them and emailed the proposal for their review, with three immediately saying "Yes!" The fourth individual agreed after reviewing the proposal in person. I truly believe the Lord had already prepared their hearts.

The first board meeting occurred November, 2014. I spoke to our new team, explaining I understood about shifting seasons. I clarified that this is our team for *establishment.* After we're up and running and if their season of service is done, that's ok! I believed the Lord would bring others to serve in other seasons.

In January, 2015, we applied for 501c3 organization, tax-exempt status. This was obtained at cost, thanks to a friend from high school who is a non-profit lawyer. Our board split the expenses. This was another blessing from the Lord. I didn't have the money upfront, but our team stepped out in faith to start the clinic as a non-profit. It was completed for one-fourth what it should have cost.

Unfailing Love Clinic opened its doors in August, 2015, ten years after my dream and five years after my vision. Nine months after our first board meeting we had supplies, finances and volunteers. Everything in the clinic was paid for and we had no debt.

Being a vessel for God's love, being able to pour that love into those needing healing would've been enough. I felt blessed to be doing what God intended me to do. The clinic became a platform to release medicine and ministry together. And yet, the Lord had more for me to accomplish.

Through many dreams and encounters with the Lord, He's shown me even greater things. Unfailing Love Clinic will be a clinic for the nations. We will be running mission teams. These teams will reach out and serve, all the while telling people that Jesus loves *them*. My future includes speaking and teaching how to discover who you were created to be; how to hear God's voice, and how to follow Him with faith.

Unfailing Love Clinic is not here to preach to people. There are enough churches and pastors to do that. It's a place where we demonstrate and become the hands and feet of Jesus. Not just by what we say, but how we treat people and even more by how we *serve.*

Although we will always ask permission to pray for individuals, it's not a requirement to receive medical services. *Pray continually. Love abandonedly. Serve generously.*

This is our mission. To serve the nations with every gift God has given us. Whether its medicine, counseling, prayer, or a combination of all three; we desire to love others with unfailing, never ending love. What does that look like? It looks like 1 John 4:19. *"We love, because He first loved us."*

Kara Mankey, FNP-C
Decatur, Indiana

* **House church**: House church or home church is a label used to describe a group of Christians who regularly gather for worship in private homes.

****Beliefs:** (1) God created this world and everything in it in six days and rested on the seventh day. (2) Jesus was born of a virgin and is the Son of God. He was crucified on the cross as our atonement for sin. Three days later He rose from the grave and promised eternal life to all who acknowledge and are in relationship with Him. (3) We believe that God, Jesus, and Holy Spirit are the Trinity, three in one. (4) The Holy Bible is the word of God. The Bible gives examples and instruction about living our lives on earth and eternal promises. (5) As followers of Jesus Christ, the Holy Spirit lives within us and empowers us to operate in the gifting of the Spirit, which release the fragrance of Jesus and allows others to encounter Him.

*****Vision Statement:** Uniting a community as one body under the head of Christ to reach out and serve the Nations.

******Goals, present:** (1) Provide education, services, and resources that empower individuals to take control of their health and be active participants in health promotion activities. (2) Unite a community of all denominations as one under the head of Christ to serve the nations. (3) Be the hands and feet of Jesus and share His love to all we encounter.

*******Goals, future:** Unfailing Love provides an opportunity for everyone in the community to reach out and serve others. A stationary free-clinic will operate three days a week in Decatur, Indiana. Medical outreaches are also operated from the clinic to promote health and well-being to the local community; extending to the desolate places around the world. Clinics will be established in other nations, beginning in Africa. Trained individuals from the local community will run the clinics and they will operate outreaches within their own communities.

Anyone wanting to donate (tax deductible) to Unfailing Love Clinic, please email: office@unfailingloveclinic.org for more information.

To hear more about Kara's story, you may purchase her book *Chasing Your Destiny* on Amazon.com.

Father Knows Best

**"Rejoice in the Lord always. And, again I say rejoice."
Philippians 4:4**

The summer of 1995, my wife drove me to the emergency room. While at a family cookout, I'd been struck in the side with a basketball. X-rays revealed I'd broken two ribs. This wasn't supposed to happen. I was 38 years old. A basketball slipping from my hands and hitting my side shouldn't have caused two ribs to break. But then again, I shouldn't have had Crohn's disease, either. I called my doctor to inform him of my newest symptom.

"I want you to come in," Dr. Steury had said. "I want to look at it."

And so, after an examination and more tests, I returned a week later for the results. "Because of the steroids you're on, I'm afraid you've developed osteoporosis," Dr. Steury said, looking at test results. "You're going to have to have surgery, or die."

I felt as if I'd just been slapped in the face. *Die?* I knew I'd been struggling in some areas, but I never considered it to be that serious. A numbness crept over my mind as I tried processing my own death. I knew the side effects of taking steroids were pretty bad, but every time I tried cutting back, my pain and diarrhea would come roaring back.

Steroids had been the only medicine that alleviated the worst of my symptoms. Chronic diarrhea, weight loss, and excruciating pain were my companions without it. Every time my symptoms stabilized, Dr. Steury would attempt to lower the dosage. My symptoms would become even worse, forcing him to up the dosage even higher than before. By this time, I'd been on a high dose of steroids for six years. I'd suffered nearly a dozen hospital stays, some for weeks, with painful infections. Still, dying was the farthest thing from my mind. I knew I'd been diagnosed with Crohn's (one in a group of conditions known as Inflammatory Bowel Disease) a few years earlier...

Flu-like symptoms which refused to go away deteriorated into severe pain, which sent me to the hospital for the first of many stays. By 8:30 p.m., I lay in my room, the light dimmed for the night. I was alone.

What I had thought was the flu would soon turn out to be something far worse. I didn't feel good. In fact, I was in a lot of pain. Looking up to the ceiling, I remember thinking, *How did I get here?* Out loud I said, "You know Lord, this just shouldn't be."

Suddenly, I heard in my mind a voice so loud and so clear, citing a Bible verse that would reverberate for years to come. *Son, You'll live and not die and declare the wonderful works of God.* I knew this verse came from Psalms 118:17, as I'd been a pastor for nearly a year.

"Okay! That's the central theme you want me to stay focused on," I said, glad for the spiritual direction. However, after thinking about it for several minutes, a new thought popped into my head. *What do you mean, I won't die? Is it that serious?*

I found the answer to that question a few days later after many tests, including a scope of my intestines. "You've got Crohn's disease." And, they began to educate me on what that was. After a week and a half they dismissed me with about five different medications, one which was prednisone. I assumed I'd be able to return to work, but it would be four months until I was healthy enough.

In October the following year, a side effect of the disease forced my return to the hospital. I'd developed a fistula, a tunnel-shaped abscess filled with infection. Roughly, forty percent of Crohn's sufferers experience fistulas. I was no different.

From my rectum to my tail-bone, the fistula had expanded to nearly an inch wide as well as high, off my skin. Besides being very painful, I suffered fever, bleeding, diarrhea, dehydration and sepsis. X-rays, (upper and lower GI series) were taken. They found ulceration, bleeding and hemorrhaging. A surgeon was called in when they discovered my white blood cell count extremely high.

However, before the decision was made to operate, the fistula began draining on its own. The doctors put me on strong antibiotics. The only relaxation I got was soaking in a bathtub. The only way I slept was with ice packs between my legs.

After two weeks, I became well enough to go home. It took six months however, for the fistula to drain. I was given the choice between Depends underwear or women's sanitary napkins to absorb the drainage. To save money I chose the latter. I quickly learned God allows no space for pride when it comes to suffering. Coincidentally, it also gave me an appreciation for what women deal with on a routine basis.

For the next few years, I experienced various side effects and set backs that sent me to the hospital nearly a dozen times. Due to high dose of steroids, my pancreas no longer produced insulin. I developed diabetic symptoms which required additional medications and a strict diet. I lost weight, dropping to 120 pounds. Though my doctor began suggesting surgery, I resisted. Every time I inquired of God whether I should or shouldn't, his words echoed in my soul, *You will live and not die...*

By now, my youngest son was four years old. I looked frail, as if I'd been through chemotherapy. He had overheard talk from family members. One day, he walked up to me and said, "Dad, are you going die?"

I said, "You don't worry about it. I'm going to be fine. God's going to take care of me. He's going to take care of you. You're going to be fine."

How do you explain to a child that God had *promised me* I wouldn't die? And so, I began taking him with me to my doctor appointments. I said to him, "I want you to see what the doctor says. I want you to see what's going on." I did it to bring him some peace. He seemed fine after that.

Not so with my siblings or my mother. My mom would call after every appointment. "What did the doctor say?" If the report was good, she'd be happy. If I had a bad report, she'd say, "You need to listen to him!"

Finally, I told her, "Mom, Doctor *Jesus* told me I'm going to be okay."

Still, she wasn't convinced. She'd put up other family members to try and persuade me from my unyielding stance against surgery. I knew it was her love for me that overrode my assurances that God had a plan and it didn't include my death.

Soon after, a new symptom emerged. I began to feel a burning sensation in my feet. This new affliction felt as if I were walking on hot coals. As it traveled up my legs, my skin became so sensitive it felt like open wounds with salt being rubbed on it. I hated to wear shoes. I hated to wear pants. But of course, I had to.

I began to feel like the woman in the Bible with an issue of blood. *"She had suffered greatly under the care of many physicians and had spent all she had, but to no avail. Instead, her condition had only grown worse."* (Mark 5:26)

Dr. Steury sent me to a neurologist. This doctor ran several tests, determining I had a chemical imbalance in my brain. I was prescribed more medicine.

"I want you to start out taking two of these, three times a day. If that doesn't work, go to three pills, three times a day. And if that doesn't work, go to four pills, three times a day. I want you to do this until you get to a dosage that works."

"Ok," I said. But thought to myself, *You probably know more than me, but I'd think you'd know how much.* Out loud, I asked, "How long do I have to be on them?"

"Oh, you'll be on these the rest of your life."

Again and again, whenever the doctors pronounced their diagnosis, from the permanence of my disease to endless medicines, God would instantly bring to mind the words he spoke my first hospital stay, *You will live and not die...* I clung to that promise, knowing without faith, I'd have no strength. I needed faith to build enough strength to fight the battle before me.

"No, I won't," I stated flatly.

Two months later, I'd just taken the last pill from the bottle the neurologist prescribed. I was about to call in my prescription so I could pick it up the next day.

And that's when I had what I call an inward witness; a *knowing.* It wasn't a voice. Some people call it a gut instinct. Having a witness is best described as a red light. Green light means, 'yes, go ahead,' while yellow light means, 'proceed with caution.' Red light means 'stop.' I felt God was telling me, *You don't need that pain medicine for your legs anymore.*

With everything I'd been through with the Lord, I trusted Him enough to follow where He led. I did not refill my prescription. True to God's witness, the burning sensations in my lower limbs disappeared.

However, the abdominal pain and relapses did take their toll. I grew discouraged and then depressed. I would pray over my medicine. I'd get to feeling better and then something else would happen. It would've been so easy to just quit and say, "Cut it out, Lord! Let me get on with my life!" But, every time I'd think about it, I would hear that voice. *No, you'll live and not die, and you'll declare the wonderful works of God.* Then, I'd change my mind, telling myself, "I'll just keep treading along."

There were times God showed me his grace. Little things he'd do along the way to remind me. After four years of chronic disease, you forget what its like to be well. One time, while taking a bath, it felt as if everything had suddenly left me. I felt strong. I felt well. It was just for an instant. I said out loud, "Lord, this is health! This is what health is!"

I had forgotten.

It was momentary, but it got my mind back onto being well, not sick. And, I felt sick every day. I had to prick my finger and measure blood sugar. It would measure 400 and I'd think, "That's not the way it's supposed to be." But, somewhere along the line, it's going to be normal. All the evidence of the lab reports, high temperatures and every setback says, "No, you're not. You're not well and you're never going to be well again."

I'd become so used to dealing with the doctors and the disease that I'd forgotten what it was like. And, if you can't imagine it, then you can't achieve it. *"Where there is no vision, people perish: but he that keepeth the law, happy is he."* (Proverbs 29:18) And, so God reminded me of the vision. *This is where we're going. Learn to enjoy the journey.*

One night in the spring of 1993, I couldn't sleep. My chest hurt and it was hard to breathe. I took pain pills from thirty minutes to four hours apart, per Dr. Steury's recommendations. After a sleepless night and thinking I was having a heart attack, I called the next morning. The doctor's office had me come in immediately. They discovered I had severe constipation due to the pain medication.

I had gained another symptom to deal with.

Through my illness, I learned what it truly means to enjoy the journey. Before, I'd always believed that I knew how I would handle adversity. "If I had to go through this or that, *this* is what I'd do. I'd just trust in God!" I'd learned that walking with God is not that easy. So many factors you never expected would factor in.

Like doubt.

When you've had so many defeats, you don't feel like getting up. You don't want to keep going. But you'd never know that last time you got up, *that* may be the last time you'll get knocked down. Its like when you tell people you've lost something, "I found it in the last place I looked."

That's because, you don't look for it anymore. You get up one more time. You don't quit, because God is seldom early. But He is faithful.

There came a time He showed his faithfulness in a powerful way. I was in bed, curled up in pain. It was about ten in the morning. My wife was home, but in another room. The Lord said to me, *I thought you believed you were healed?*

I said, "I *do* believe it. I believe that by the striped body of Jesus, I'm healed. I believe the word of God. I believe the Bible. I even believe the cover. It says Holy Bible. I believe the Bible is holy."

He said, *Well, people aren't in bed at this time.*

"But, you don't understand," I said. "I'm in pain. I couldn't straighten up and get dressed if I wanted to."

A few minutes pass by, and again He says, *I thought you said you believed you were healed?*

"I do believe it. I believe the word of God," and I went through it again.

Well, people at 10 o'clock in the morning, aren't in bed at this time.

I lay there in bed, again telling Him what all's going on. "I'm in so much pain. Unless I'm going to get up and take a bunch of pain pills, I can't straighten up if I wanted to."

A third time He said, *People aren't in bed at this time.*

And, then it dawned on me. "Oh! You want me to get up!"

So, I said, "Ok. I'll try." It took me thirty minutes to slide over to the side of the bed, get my pants on as well as the rest of my clothes.

"Ok, I'm dressed," I said.

Now, go to work.

I'm still feeling terrible. But, I walk out of the bedroom. My wife Camelia, says, "Where are you going?"

"I'm going to the office."

"I thought you weren't feeling well. Are you feeling better?"

"No," I said as I walked out and got into the car.

Our church is in the country, and we lived only three miles away. As I got within a quarter mile of church, I had to pull over and vomit. However, once I got there and went into my office, I dropped into my chair.

"Whew! I made it!"

As soon as the words left my mouth, I realized I had no pain. Now, the pain would later return. But God had taught me a lesson. *God is faithful, if we follow Him.* He wasn't telling me I couldn't take pain pills. If God hadn't spoken those words to me repeatedly, I'd have lain there, doubled over, not understanding my assignment. He was addressing my lack of trust in His faithfulness to me.

In the spring or early summer of 1994, a second fistula sent me to the hospital. It was identical in every way; the position, the infection and the pain. I knew to expect more blood tests, more scopes, more X-Rays.

The next morning, when Dr. Steury came to see me, I was feeling much better. "You must have people praying for you," he said.

"As a matter of fact, I do."

"Yesterday, when you arrived, your white blood count was 35,000. This morning, it's 14,000, which is on the high side of normal."

"Great! Can I go home?"

"I want to take some more blood and we will see what your numbers are after that."

After my overnight stay, I went home on antibiotics that afternoon. Camilla drove me home. I looked at the hospital's reflection in the side mirror of the car. I was tired of being sick. I was tired of hospitals. I was tired of tests and medications.

"I'll never go back into there again," I stated firmly. "Not for this."

With that announcement, I finally drove my stake of faith into the ground. I wasn't telling God what to do. I wasn't putting Him in a box or demanding He heal me, or let me die. I was claiming my trust in His Word. It was a stake where I could measure from now on.

There were no fireworks; no sudden healing. My disease continued. However, something in me had changed. I began to rejoice over every victory, no matter how small. I found when I remained focused on the little things; they grew large, becoming my strength. With that strength, I realized I could endure anything.

I watched my diet and tried staying active, which meant I didn't need as much diabetic medicine anymore. I'd stopped taking medicine for the pain in my feet and legs. With every victory, I rejoiced. However, I was still on large doses of prednisone.

I saw Dr. Steury every three months. We had a routine that always started with him reviewing my medicines and my level of steroids. If my symptoms were under control, he'd have me cut back on the prednisone. Within 24 hours, I'd relapse with diarrhea, nausea and dehydration. Without pain medicine, I'd be curled in the fetal position in excruciating pain. In order to control the symptoms I had to continue taking steroids. It remained a vicious cycle for years.

And then I developed osteoporosis and broke two ribs.

"Because of the steroids you're on, I'm afraid you've developed osteoporosis," Dr. Steury said, looking at the test results. "You're going to have to have surgery, or die."

I felt as if I'd just been slapped in the face. *Die?* I knew I'd been struggling in some areas, but I never considered it to be that serious. Feeling numb, I could barely think.

"Wait a minute," I said. "What do you mean?"

"The disease is killing you. And the medicine is killing you. You're not going to be able to tolerate this if your bones are that fragile. You could fall and break an arm. I know we've talked about it before. But, you really need to consider this."

And just like the other times doctor Steury recommended surgery, the words the Lord had spoke to me burst from my mouth. "No! I'll live and *not* die. I'll declare the wonderful works of God."

I then told him, "The Bible says the word of God is the anchor to your soul, (Hebrews 6:19) and every time I get to a place that's shaky or when I start doubting, that word rises up and anchors my soul. And, God told Joshua, 'If you meditate upon my word day and night, and observe and do all that's written there, and then you'll make your way that's successful.'" (Joshua 1:8)

In my mind, I'm thinking, "God told me *I'd live and not die*, so dying isn't on the table. And neither is surgery on the table. The only option left is that God is going to come through for me." I shook my head. "I just can't go that way."

Dr. Steury remained gentle and patient, having heard my words before. "I'm setting you up for a second opinion."

"Why?" I asked.

"I've done everything I can do except for you to have surgery. And, you don't want that." And then he added, "If I give you a second opinion, it may help you to decide."

"I believe what you're telling me. I don't need a second opinion," I said. "But, I'll go."

A week after the second doctor's visit, I'd returned to Dr. Steury's office. When he entered the exam room, the report was in his hands. "This is the report. Here, you read it," he said, handing it to me.

When I looked up from reading, he continued. "He's saying the same thing I am."

"I see that," I said, nodding.

"So, what do you want to do? If you don't want to go to Cleveland, we could probably send you to Indiana University."

By this time, I'd begun putting on weight. I was no longer weak. I could work. I looked healthy and felt good; that is, until I tried cutting down on steroids. Only then, would I experience symptoms and pain.

I said, "You know what I want to do. I want you to help me *maintain.*"

"Okay," Dr. Steury said. "That door is open whenever you want."

By February of 1997, I was being monitored every three weeks. Dr. Steury finally insisted, "If you're not going to have surgery, we *have* to get you off the steroids."

I knew this to be true. Yet, the last time we tried cutting back, all my symptoms had returned. Thus, I was back to 100 milligrams of prednisone. I would have to cut my steroid dosage before my next office visit.

I was nervous about what was about to happen. I wasn't in pain at the moment, so I hadn't taken any pain medication lately. Always, in the back of my mind, there was that thought, that fear that once I cut back on the steroids, the pain would return.

So, keeping my pain meds with me had been my security blanket. And then, a week before my next scheduled visit with Dr. Steury, it happened.

I was in Broken Arrow, Oklahoma attending a Bible Seminar. It was 10 p.m. My wife and I had just returned to our hotel room. I had both prednisone and pain medication with me, which at the time was a combination of Tylenol and codeine. As I started to take the pain meds, I heard the Lord speak to me. *You no longer need that.*

I was apprehensive at first, but then I grew excited. If the Lord was telling me I didn't need pain medicine, I should soon have full healing.

Just as quickly, my mind went back to the times I'd thought I didn't need it anymore only to be disappointed when my pain returned. I was 750 miles from home. It was a twelve to fourteen hour drive back. Pain was the last thing I wanted.

I sat on the edge of my bed trying to resist fearful thoughts. "You've never told me to do something that wasn't in my best interest. You've proven Yourself faithful over and over again. So, at Your Word, I *don't* need this pain medication."

I didn't take it. And I rejoiced on the drive home, because I didn't need it.

Two weeks later, I awoke and ate breakfast. I always took the prednisone with food or else I'd become nauseas. I was about to take my morning dosage when I heard the Lord speak again. *You no longer need that. Quit taking it!* I heard it so loudly and with such authority, I knew in my heart that I didn't need it and would never need it anymore.

However, *fear* tried talking me out of it. *Do you remember how many times you tried to quit taking this over the years? You failed at it over and over again! What makes you think this time is any different?*

Then I recalled how, just a few weeks earlier, the Lord had told me I didn't need pain meds anymore and I hadn't used them since. Now, He's telling me I don't need the prednisone. All throughout this struggle with Crohn's, He told me *I'd live and not die, and declare the wonderful works of the Lord.* He had proven Himself faithful and trustworthy.

So I said, "I choose to trust You with my life."

I knew I had a doctor's appointment in a week. If I my symptoms returned, I could always go back on the prednisone. Somewhere in the back of my mind, I half-expected something to happen by the next day.

Nothing did. I then expected symptoms within 48 hours of stopping the prednisone. But after two days, I realized, "Darn! I think God's right!"

I couldn't wait to see Dr. Steury.

The visit was like every other visit. I sat in the waiting room until the nurse called me. I was weighed, then taken to a room to measure my pulse and blood pressure. Before leaving, she took notes of my medications.

Dr. Steury came in a few minutes later. "How are we doing today?"

"I'm doing *great!*"

He took a seat, opening my file. "How much of the prednisone are you currently taking? Were you able to cut it back?"

"I'm not taking any."

He looked at the nurse's notes. "The last time I saw you, which was about three weeks ago, you were taking 100 milligrams. Did you cut *all* of that down?"

"No," I said. "I *quit* taking them last week. At that time, I was still on 100 milligrams."

Dr. Steury's jaw dropped open. "You're not taking *any?*" he asked, clearly shocked.

"No, I'm not."

"How are you doing?"

"I'm doing well."

"You're the first person I've ever heard of that's ever been able to do that," he said. "And, this is why. Prednisone is similar to a hormone that's made in your adrenal glands. Once you take it for a while, your body quits producing it. If you don't wean yourself slowly, it causes severe pain and weakness. Your blood pressure can drop really low, or go very high. It can even cause strokes."

"I feel fine," I said.

"Still, I'm going examine you and then run some tests to see what's going on. You're feeling well and we don't want to do anything to mess that up."

A week or so later, I'd returned to hear what my test results were. "Here's your clean bill of health," doctor said, handing me the papers. The pages were filled with numbers and words I couldn't pronounce. "This is what our goal for you was," he said, pointing. "And, this is what you've reached."

All my test results were normal.

He then sat down, making notes in my file. "I don't think I'll need to see you again unless you have problems." All at once, Dr. Steury smiled. "I'm so glad you didn't listen to us."

The words slipped out of my mouth before I realized it. "I'm so glad I didn't listen to you either. And, I don't mean any disrespect by that."

What I felt, was thankful and grateful to my Lord Jesus Christ. Although there's currently no cure for Crohn's, I've been symptom free for the past twenty years.

Faith isn't something seen with the eyes or proven with our senses. The only concrete evidence we have his His Word. And so with all things involving faith, we wrestle with it. There's plenty of room for doubt. I had experienced and fully understood my own struggles. It would've been so much easier to just do what the doctor's recommended. Common sense may tell you to go one way. But if it contradicts where God is leading you and you give in to the pressure, you may miss the blessings along His path.

Once I eliminated the fear of death, I began to appreciate the little things. I discovered it's the little things that life is all about. It's not about things we collect or gather. It's about people. Invest in your family today, because tomorrow you may not get a chance to.

When I was young, I was busy establishing a career by starting a church while working a secular job. I was gone a lot. I took my wife and kids for granted. Pain however, gets your attention. It took God sending me on my journey to show me what's important. No matter how painful that journey may be, there's beauty if you just stop and look around.

Bad things can come to good people. That's life. But, if you enjoy the journey no matter how painful, you will receive strength. The word enjoy comes from the word joy. In Philippians 4:4, Paul said, *"Rejoice in the Lord. And, again I say, rejoice."*

Why did he have to tell the Philippian church to rejoice? Obviously, it had to be in a time they didn't feel like rejoicing. If everything is good, it's easy to rejoice. You don't have to tell someone to rejoice. But, there's something spiritual about it when you rejoice through a bad situation.

And Nehemiah says, *"The joy of the Lord is your strength."* (Nehemiah 8:10) It's difficult to fight a fight of faith without any strength. Not only does this verse put us in remembrance to God's faithfulness, but it calls us to *voice* it. Every time you voice it to yourself or others, it's like telling God, "I love you."

What do you do when you find yourself at a physical or spiritual crossroads? Find a scripture that's meaningful to you, to your situation. Find that rock you can stand on. Meditate on it. Let the Spirit of God, who is the spirit of truth show you where that scripture's going to take you.

How do you know if a scripture is meant for you and not for those at the time it was written? Jesus says, "The words I have spoken to you are spirit and life." (John 6:63) He made it personal. So, when you have the experience of scripture jumping out at you like you've been slapped in the face, that's God making it personal. For you.

I'm not suggesting anyone ignore medical advice. God is the author of medicine and He heals in many different ways. I gladly used the available medicines available to me until the Lord indicated otherwise.

No one can predict the outcome of a healing *in the natural.* Only God knows what our journey is and what it's meant to teach. All I can say is whatever your journey, whatever your circumstances, always listen to our heavenly Father.

Because, Father knows best.

Pastor Anthony Robles
Harvest Time Bible Church
Geneva, Indiana

I Hear You

"In my distress I called out to the LORD; I cried to my God for help. From his temple he heard my voice; my cry came before him, into his ears." Psalm 18:6

I had begun to read the Bible before falling asleep at night. I'd prop myself in bed and spend time reacquainting myself with scripture I hadn't studied in a while. It was the one activity I knew to do despite the many things I had been doing wrong. At age twenty-nine, I was a divorced mother of two living in a new town with a new job. My life had not turned out like I'd planned and in fact, seemed heading in the wrong direction. My marriage and my Christian walk had become a colossal failure. And, I'd just lost the new love of my life to another woman.

Eleven years before, I'd married my sweetheart out of high school. The first three years were wonderful, or so I thought. After the birth of our second daughter, everything changed. My husband began to drink. As time went on it became a daily occurrence. And so did the arguments. It seemed as if both of us had changed and we'd grown apart.

I always believed marriage was a lifetime commitment. You didn't enter into it lightly and you never left except under dire circumstances. When our relationship became strained, I often prayed for God to save our marriage. I didn't want to become a statistic. I abhorred the title *divorcee*. When our marriage ended anyway and the divorce papers signed, I couldn't believe God had failed to answer my prayers.

I'd moved away to a new town and a new job. I also found a new church. I'd given my life into God's hands, asking Him to take control. Except that I still held back one specific area. My romantic life. I felt as if He'd failed me in my last time of need. And even though I'd given to God every other aspect of my life; that was the one area I refused Him entrance. Still, I desperately wanted a stable life and that meant getting remarried. I had decided to find a husband on my own.

I'd still pray about it, of course. I wasn't such a fool to not even *ask*. But, whenever I considered dating someone, I never viewed them through the lens of Christian values. My decisions were based solely on worldly perspectives. Could they provide for us? Could we get along? Would they make me happy? I didn't dare venture beyond that; even if that meant putting myself in imprudent, unchaste situations. If I found them attractive, they didn't drink to excess and made enough money, I would be happy. I prayed for the end result while leaving God out of the choice of *who*. My reason? I imagined God might provide someone righteous, but surely *unattractive,* right? I mean, God didn't care about those things, did He? I was afraid He'd choose someone I wouldn't want to marry. I convinced myself He'd let me do the picking if I wanted. Besides, I'd been divorced for eight years and I was tired of waiting.

The one thing I knew I'd done right is find a good church for me and my girls. I loved my new church! They focused more on the Bible than my previous church. The pastor strongly encouraged everyone to read from it daily. He even recommended finding a Bible with wide margins so we could write on them. So I purchased an NIV and studied it whenever

I could. With young children, that usually meant after they'd been put to bed.

As I settled in, I opened my Bible to the Old Testament and began reading. As my eyes fell upon Isaiah 59:2 I suddenly felt the sharp stab of condemnation. *"But your iniquities have separated you from your God; your sins have hidden his face from you, so that he will not hear."*

I stared at the verse, reading it again.

At that moment I believed God had declared my prayers had been falling on deaf ears. Because I hadn't conducted my life piously, He had refused to listen. Nor, would He help me in any way. I had thought I could pick and choose what to pray for and how I should get it. *Yes, I want this result; no, You can't be involved except to make it happen.*

This verse seemed to contradict my belief that God would overlook my behavior while I pursued relationships. It felt as if a ton of bricks had fallen on my chest. I couldn't breathe. I envisioned God literally turning his face away whenever I called upon Him, my voice muted; my prayers refused. All those years of hoping and praying, chasing and being chased had been wasted. I knew instantly, without God I'd never obtain the desires of my heart.

Suddenly weeping, I cried out loud, "God, can you hear me? Do you even *hear me?*"

...   .

The 1980's was the era of the Cold War and the birth of the Yuppie generation. MTV exploded inside the music industry and cable news brought world crises into my living room. Like my failed marriage, everything seemed chaotic. And lonely. I desperately wanted a companion. Besides, I needed a father figure for my daughters.

I told myself I needed to meet men where they could be found. In my limited experience, that nearly always meant bars. Though my conscience whispered it's not where I would find a godly man, my louder, flesh person declared I'd be able to find one anyway. Except, I kept failing. Miserably. After several relationships had run aground, I set my sights on one who seemed to have it all. Scott. Though we met in a bar, he went to church. He was handsome, fun and interesting. He had a successful business. Perfect! It was a match made in heaven, crafted by me.

I had been praying, no *begging*, for God to grant me this one thing.

Yet, it wasn't as perfect as I thought. There were unresolved issues on both our parts. Our relationship was unstable, his commitment shaky. I had unrealistic expectations and abandonment issues. He had recently broken up with a woman he had wanted to marry. Despite all that, I believed with enough time Scott would see we were meant to be. We got along well. We never argued. I expected his hesitation to get involved in a steady relationship would eventually go away.

I was sure Scott was *The One* and pursued him unashamedly. After two years of on and off dating, I experienced a set back when he chose to start dating another. We still remained friendly, and in my mind, that link was enough to withstand this newest threat. I had already outlasted his past attempts to regain his old girlfriend; surely he'd soon realize I was the prize he sought. I made sure we ran into each other in church and elsewhere *accidentally on purpose*. With perseverance and determination, I believed I'd win out.

Besides, I was now going to church regularly and praying about it. In fact, whenever I ran for exercise, I prayed. Running had become my coping mechanism. It was a constant in my unstable life. I rarely remember a time where I didn't feel off kilter. From the death of a parent and harsh family life, to marriage, motherhood and then divorce; I never quite recovered from one incident before another seemed to befall.

With each failed relationship I grew more desperate. I wanted, no—I needed—to find someone to lean on. I'd always been the strong one for others. At the end of my rope, I'd found Scott. Surely, God had brought us together! I felt certain he was the man to provide everything I needed. All I had to do was to wait for his new relationship to fail.

During that time, I received strong feelings that God was telling me to back off from any contact with Scott. I grew excited. Surely, this meant something was about to happen. My fears calmed. God was working this out for my good! I anticipated Scott breaking up with his new girlfriend and then contacting me.

But soon after, I read in the papers of a romantic proposal between a local couple involving a hot air balloon and "Will You Marry Me?" written on the ground. When I read further, I felt devastated! My guy, who I just *knew* would be my next husband, had gotten engaged to someone else.

I was crushed. I couldn't stop crying. How had this happened? What was God *doing?* To make matters worse, Scott brought his fiancé to the same church services, sitting in the pew behind me. I often had to shake her hand. The pain was nearly unbearable as I'd fight to keep my composure. I knew it wasn't her fault. She hadn't known about me. Scott never told her I was his old girlfriend.

My conscience whispered that if I hadn't gotten ahead of myself, I wouldn't now be suffering. I'd done this to myself. I was only suffering the consequences of my own actions. I hadn't waited on God to provide a companion because I hadn't trusted Him. But, I was still angry. And if a person could have a spiritual temper tantrum, I was having a full blown episode that lasted for months.

While laying in bed reading the Bible, all those thoughts haunted me. God is all powerful. He could've granted my prayers, but He hadn't. I couldn't understand why I'd lost Scott to another. And then, I stumbled across Isaiah 59:2. In an instant I knew. God had turned away from me! My *sins* had kept Him from being able to help. It had been my stubborn refusal to allow God that part of my life because I thought I knew more than He did.

I'd just blown my last chance at happiness! It was all my fault.

Every pain, every loss I'd experienced in life seemed to cascade inside my mind. I recalled my father's death, to the death of my marriage as well as every relationship since. Every happiness I'd ever possessed, had been snatched away too soon. I felt retched. It was too much to bear! Had they all been my fault?

"God, can you hear me? Do you even hear me?" had tumbled from my mouth.

All at once, my heart unexpectedly expanded with feelings of indescribable joy. I heard in my mind, *I hear you and I'll take care of it.* I was astounded. I felt ecstatic! God had literally leaned down to whisper in my ear words of comfort. My happiness was overwhelming. God heard me! He would take care of it!

However, over the next two weeks, doubt crept in. Did I imagine it? Had that really been God speaking or only something I wanted to hear? During my morning run, I again prayed about it. I asked God, "Was it really You? Did you talk to me?" Once again, the same words echoed in my heart. *I hear you and I'll take care of it.* I burst into tears, saying over and over, "Thank you, God! Thank You!"

I finally accepted that I wasn't going to do the "choosing" anymore. God had finally broken my stubborn will. I would have to be obedient or I'd continue to experience pain and disappointment. I realized that God didn't want just a part of me. He wanted all of me. He needed to be in control, even in areas of love and marriage. Either I was completely committed to God or I wasn't. So, I stopped seeking out those who I thought were right for me. Anyone who asked me out learned on our first date I was no longer *that kind of woman*. I had very few second dates.

I now regularly read my Bible. I underlined verses that held meaning. When I ran across, *"The righteous cry out, and the LORD hears them; he delivers them from all their troubles. The lord is close to the brokenhearted and saves those who are crushed in spirit." (Psalms 34: 17-18),* I believed He truly understood my brokenness. He had used that experience to break my will, but not my spirit. The pain had been necessary to get my attention. I would simply have to wait for Him to fulfill His promise.

Over the next two years, I played and replayed those words over and over, wondering to myself, *when? When is God going to take care of it?* I recalled a preacher once saying we're to remind God of His promises. So I figured, well, this is a promise *to me*. I should be able to remind Him. And I did; often and with gusto. "Remember God, You promised! You said you heard me and that you'd take care of it!" Though it may have been silly, it always made me feel better.

Those two years turned out to be necessary because that was the time I needed to repair certain parts of my life. If I wanted to attract a godly man, I needed to be a godly woman. That meant walking the walk while trusting God to bring us together. I would also accept whomever He chose.

Funny thing happened. God, being the God of love and romance knew what my heart hoped for. He had wanted to give me someone I desired all along. And, He did! After two years of being faithful, God fulfilled His promise. Not only did Russell turn out to be godly, he was also attractive in every way. When we first met, I suddenly realized this man wouldn't have chosen the old me or my former lifestyle. God had made me a new creation! My act of obedience had literally changed my life.

Needless to say, Russell and I eventually married. I'm far happier than I ever imagined I'd be. I've been blessed with more children and a satisfying career. Looking back, I can see how my current husband is a more suitable choice than the man I thought I wanted to marry. God knew better.

I've learned many things. God loves me enough to deny giving me that which I shouldn't have. He loves me through my anger and sorrow. I now understand my former neediness was misplaced. Instead of looking for completeness from a man, I should have been seeking it from God. Only then would I be ready for a healthy relationship.

It wasn't until later I realized why we are told to remind God of his promises. It has nothing to do with making sure He doesn't forget and everything about reminding ourselves. *God didn't need reminding. I did!*

Lastly, through my walk with the Lord, I now know it's not God who ever turns away from his children. It's those with an unrepentant heart who turn away from Him. Upon further reading, I finally finished Isaiah, Chapter 59. The 21st verse said it all. *"'As for me, this is my covenant with them,' says the LORD. 'My Spirit, who is on you, will not depart from you, and my words that I have put in your mouth will always be on your lips, on the lips of your children and on the lips of their descendants—from this time on and forever,' says the LORD."*

Never again will I worry about God turning away or abandoning me. I've learned to wait on Him. Every desire, every request I now take to Him. After all, He knows what's best.

The Bible verses that are especially meaningful to me are: *"Delight yourself in the LORD and he will give you the desires of your heart."* Psalms 37:4

"For I know the plans I have for you." Declares the LORD, "plans to prosper you and not to harm you, plans to give you hope and a future. Then you will call upon me and come and pray to me and I will listen to you." Jeremiah 29: 11-13

"I will repay you for the years the locusts have eaten—" Joel 2:25

He had indeed heard me. And, He had taken care of it.

Bianca McCormick
Columbus, Ohio

Opening the Floodgates

"Will a mere mortal rob God? Yet you rob me. But you ask, 'How are we robbing you?' In tithes and offerings. You are under a curse—your whole nation—because you are robbing me. Bring the whole tithe into the storehouse, that there may be food in my house. Test me in this, says the Lord Almighty, and see if I will not throw open the floodgates of heaven and pour out so much blessing that there will be not room enough to store it." Malachi 3: 8-10

I got into my truck, packed with my oldest daughter's belongings. I planned on driving from Indianapolis to Valparaiso in northwest Indiana, about an hour's drive from Chicago. She had just landed her first full time teaching position. And although I was excited and relieved she now had dependable income, I was still anxious about her moving to a town where she knew no one. It was August, 2010, and it was hot.

My husband Dave would be driving the moving van, accompanied by my daughter and her boyfriend. Since he'd be taking the lead, I didn't worry about directions. I knew there'd be a long day of unloading once we got there, so I was looking forward to a relaxing drive.

After settling into my seat, I turned on the radio. I wasn't familiar with the stations in central Indiana, so I flipped through the channels until I found a clear signal. I am a radio person. Anytime I'm driving, the radio is on. Normally I listen to music. However, I recognized the voice of a well known financial advisor. It was the first channel that came in clearly and so I decided to listen to his program. As the van pulled away from the curb, I fell in behind.

The subject of financial advice attracted me. In fact, I'd had difficulty in that area most of my life. So, when he uttered the term "debt free," my ears perked up. I began listening with intensity as those who called in described their financial problems. As they recounted their difficulties, I mentally checked off my issues alongside theirs. They were describing everything I did!

I felt as if I were looking in a mirror.

Immediately, I thought of my husband Dave. I recalled how for years we struggled financially because of my spending. An image of him sitting down to pay bills arose along with the mutters and grumbles that always ensued. At times we fought. Yet despite my best attempts at controlling my spending habits, nothing ever fixed our situation.

I felt filled with remorse. I couldn't believe what I had done to him for all these years. I loved Dave. He didn't deserve this. I couldn't *do* this to him anymore! "You've got to stop this!" I said to myself. "God will help me and its time."

I knew something had to change. *I* had to change. I'd tried before, but failed. Perhaps, I'd been going about it all wrong. As a Christian, I knew God transformed people. I'd even prayed about my spending habits. And for a time, I seemed to control things. But those times never lasted. I even knew when the root of my addiction became planted. Could God change a lifetime of hurt and bewilderment? With sudden clarity, I felt God was opening the door to accomplish what I couldn't.

Growing up, I was raised in a home where my father controlled the money. My mother had to account for every penny she spent. We lived within a strict budget. Because of that, anything she purchased had to be used, on sale, or an item she could refurbish. It's difficult as a child not having the clothing or things other kids had. Making matters worse, I went to school with children of affluent doctors and lawyers. I looked with longing at their stylish clothes and listened as they recounted their vacations during spring break. Though my family wasn't actually poor, I looked and I *felt* poor.

As a consequence, I didn't believe that I was as good as they were. I was somehow less. Over time, the images of my self worth became twisted and bent. And so did the cure. If living on a budget meant I was poor, *and therefore unworthy,* I wanted nothing to do with any of that.

I married at age twenty one and for the first five years, I spent whatever I earned. It was my money. Spending made me happy. Spending money on myself and others gave me value. Buying things meant I could afford them. When our girls came along I became a stay at home mom, something I'd always wanted. And though our income had dropped, my spending hadn't.

To compensate, I began using credit cards.

Over the next two years the bills became so high, I had to admit my mistake of overspending. I got a part time job. After a year, I'd paid them down and was able to quit. You'd have thought that after quitting my job I would've changed my habits. But they'd become too deeply ingrained. By the time our kids were in middle school, our bills had become too much of a burden. Dave had announced, "You're going to have to get a full time job." And so, I went back to work.

Not only did I continue to spend and use credit cards, I began to collect things like Precious Moments. And, I didn't have just one. I had twenty. I collected silly things, like Pez's. I started buying every Pez I saw. It became a chase. "Oh, I don't have this one!" "I have that one, but not *this* one." "I'm going have every single one that's out there!"

I bought things I didn't need. A friend began collecting Beanie Babies. Now I had to have them. It wasn't just one or two. I wasn't satisfied with a few. I couldn't have what I wanted as a child, so by golly I was going to have every single one of them!

The arguments over money increased. Our bank account remained drained after every pay period. Often, we had overdrafts. I'd see how stressed my husband was and would try to stop spending. But then, our car would break down or an appliance would fail. Because we had no savings, our only solution was using a credit card.

To make matters worse, I was a giving person. God created me to be generous. I like to help people. I like to give. Many times, my spending was the result of filling needs in other people's lives. Not a bad thing when finances are under control. For me, it became another area where money was recklessly spent.

For twenty-five years we lived on the edge. And, although credit cards were our fallback resource, we developed other coping mechanisms. At pivotal times, Dave would get a raise or an unexpected bonus. We learned we could sell off two weeks of his paid vacation to get cash. We had Christmas and vacation clubs with money directly deposited. However, I would withdraw funds from time to time. Dave never knew.

The vacations we did take were as inexpensive as we could make them. For years we went camping. As I matured as a Christian, I realized I had a problem. After a day of shopping, I'd come home feeling bad. I'd go to the Lord and talk to Him about it. As my faith grew, I began praying before I went shopping. Quite often, those prayers were answered because I'd find items on sale or maybe I didn't spend as much. Or, I wouldn't spend anything.

But, I couldn't maintain consistency. I refused to be on a *budget*. A budget meant you were poor. A budget *controlled* you. And, if I had ever looked deep enough in myself, I would've known that at my core I was rebelling against being controlled. Without realizing it, compensating for my child-hood insecurities had morphed into sin. And, that's how I managed my money throughout 33 years of marriage.

Until that day.

When the radio host spoke to his callers it was as if God was speaking to me. My heart became convicted. I knew that my behavior had to stop and there was a better way. Here was the answer and God put it right there. I got very emotional.

For two and a half hours I sat glued to the radio. I listened to people who'd used biblical principles with their finances. When callers had achieved their debt free status they were allowed to shout out over the airwaves, "We're debt free!"

When I got out of the truck, I wasn't the same person who had gotten in. Something in me had changed. I couldn't wait to tell Dave because I knew he'd be excited to hear what I was going to say. We were going to go to classes together to learn how to manage our money.

And we did. I looked up where those next classes were being held. We were delighted to discover it just happened to be at Emmanuel Community Church which was less than a mile from our house.

Our very first class we learned one piece of information that once we followed it, allowed us to pay $8,000 worth of debt within four months. (We temporarily redirected retire-ment fund payments to pay down debt, starting with our lowest bills.) We were hooked! We also felt hope. We knew this was where we were supposed to be. This was the answer.

Overnight, I'd stopped using credit. We paid everything with cash. We followed a budget. And because God had chosen that moment to answer my prayers, I'd lost all desire to buy all that *stuff.* I felt healed. But the real work was yet to come. We still had to dig ourselves out of debt.

Dave worked an additional three years to pay off our mortgage, making double house payments. When necessary, we used our emergency savings fund to make repairs and purchase used cars when ours wore out. We learned to apply money management principles to our life which gave us the freedom to thrive and even go on mission trips.

There's more to the story, however. Without knowing it, God had been working on me and my finances long before I heard the radio program. He'd begun the process years before. When we joined St. Michael Evangelical Church, we were just eight years into our marriage. At the time, we weren't giving to the church like we should. After attending for five years, Pastor Bob Bruckner had invited the congregation to participate in the "Bruckner Challenge." It was based off Malachi 3: 8-10. He challenged everyone who wasn't currently tithing to begin with a two percent tithe, increasing the amount by an additional two percent each year until they reached ten percent. He promised anyone who tithed for the next three months, what bills couldn't be paid because of tithing, *he* would pay!

We realized that by not tithing, we had been robbing God for those first five years! From that point on, we took the challenge. We started immediately at the ten percent mark. It was hard! We had no savings and we barely paid our bills.

By some miracle we stayed faithful in our giving. And as I look back, I see the ways in which God had kept the promises of Deuteronomy 28, that if we're obedient in faith, He'll take care of us. That first year of tithing, when one of our daughters needed a bike, someone gave us a bicycle. We also won tickets to the circus that year. Additionally, Dave won a drawing at work for an overnight stay at a hotel for a weekend getaway. Now skeptics could claim simple coincidence. But, I saw it as proof of God fulfilling his promises.

There were other instances, like the time we had no money for groceries. That very day, I received an unanticipated insurance check that just covered our needs. Other times, when we simply had no way to pay a bill, the solution arrived in the form of a surprise bonus or an unexpected raise. But the gold standard of God's generosity was the fulfillment of a dream I'd kept for many years.

Most parents grasp the wonders and joy Disney bestows upon young girls. I was no different. It had always been my dream to take our daughters to Disney World in Orlando. If we ever did, we could afford it only once and so it had to be at an age when both could remember. In my mind, that meant one would be eight and the other ten years old. However, our finances were never great, and as that time approached I realized we were not going to be able to realize that dream.

That was the year the post office where Dave worked decided to give a bonus. It was the best Christmas present God could've given me! We were able to fly down, stay with our parents who lived nearby, and go to Disney World. I'd also wanted souvenirs for everyone and calculated a hundred dollars each would more than cover it. I can't tell you how it happened, but we ended up with an extra $400 to spend on souvenirs!

That is Grace.

No matter the circumstance no matter how many times I failed, God always came through. God proved his faithfulness for us in so many ways in spite of my sinful nature. I didn't deserve it. But, He always offers His forgiveness and mercy. I truly believe He blessed us because we were obedient in tithing. Giving back to Him what is His. He blesses that. He keeps His promises.

Today we are debt free. We have more money than we've ever had in our lives even though our income hasn't changed. We still pay with cash. We're finally in a position to be as generous as the Lord intended us to be. In fact, we recently donated a car to someone in need. God has given us more than we ever imagined and we are truly grateful.

When others ask us how we became debt free, we're eager to explain how God put a financial system in front of us to follow. Motivated by biblical principles, we acquired management tools that allowed us to become debt free while still living generously.

But, the most important lesson of all was learning that without tithing, we were robbing God. Without that commitment, without acknowledging that the money we earned was still Gods, we'd always be a slave to debt. Once we did, He placed us on the road that ultimately led to the day I sat in that car listening to a radio program.

And somewhere along the way I had a revelation. I realized my spending problem couldn't be blamed on my father. He'd simply managed family finances in ways he believed best. It was me who internalized budgeting as bad. Over time, this internal pressure manifested itself as anxiety, worry, depression and more spending. What had begun as rebellious spending had evolved into a reckless lifestyle that only I could stop.

You might think this is the end of my story, but not quite! I've recently decided it was time to get rid of all the stuff I'd accumulated. I didn't want it. I didn't need it anymore. It only reminded me of all my stupid and selfish spending. And yet, getting rid of everything I'd bought felt like I was getting rid of a part of me.

The answer came in the form of a book, *The Joy of Less*. "If something you own isn't making you smile, give it to somebody and enjoy the smile on somebody's face." So I learned how to process releasing this stuff.

I've learned many things. Not least of which is putting my life experiences in perspective. Together, my husband and I have grounded ourselves in scripture that literally came alive and jumped off the pages. Every time I come across them, it reaffirms how much God desires our freedom from anything that hinders. I gladly share them whenever I can.

"The earth is the LORD'S, and everything in it, the world, and all who live in it;" Psalm 24:1

"The rich rule over the poor, and the borrower is slave to the lender." Proverbs 22:7

"Delight yourself in the LORD, and he will give you the desires of your heart." Psalms 37:4

And the Beanie Babies? I'm saving them for my grandbabies.

Karen Kuehnert
Fort Wayne, Indiana

Acceptance

"In my Father's house are many mansions; if it were not so, I would have told you. I go to prepare a place for you." John 14:2

I walked the length of Big Beach in Maui, and then followed a little known path over lava rocks to Little Beach. Here, the locals could enjoy sand and surf away from vacationers that flocked to the other, well-known vacation spot. I would spend a day of bodysurfing on this windy but beautiful day in May.

The waves were really high, which made perfect conditions for board surfers. However, due to the accompanying undertow, life guards on Big Beach had warned swimmers to stay out of the water. *That's for people who don't know how to swim,* I thought.

I on the other hand, considered myself a very good swimmer. In fact, I'd been swimming most of my life. At age 32, I was physically strong. I could run for miles. I'd rigorously trained in kick-boxing. And on top of all that, I practiced Pilates and yoga.

Besides, I was now on a beach *without* life guards.

Bodysurfing doesn't require a board. Your body becomes your board as you catch oncoming waves. When you see a wave you want to ride, you turn your back to it and push off from the ocean bottom. You then launch into a front crawl swim, making big scoops with your hands and kicking as fast as you can. As soon as the wave lifts, you stop kicking and thrust one or both arms in the direction you want to go. Taking a big breath you stiffen and align your entire body into a downward diagonal. You can then experience the exhilaration of a sport that's as pure as it gets. It's just you and the ocean. Your body is your equipment; your technique determines the amount of thrill.

I wasn't reckless by nature though, and remained cautious while surfing. I didn't want to get sucked out to sea. And for the first half hour everything seemed fine. Suddenly, in what I thought was waist deep water, a big wave came from nowhere. Towering twenty feet above my head, it crashed into me, pushing me beneath the water. When I surfaced, I found myself further from the beach. I quickly calculated I'd been driven leftward, in a northwest direction.

I immediately began to swim toward shore. I wasn't concerned for I was less than 75 yards away. However, another large wave hit, sending me tumbling to the bottom. The water's force raked me over sharp lava, cutting me. Again I surfaced, finding myself even further out.

A few people on the beach took notice. They stood staring in my direction while I swam. My confidence began to wane as wave after wave propelled me into the sanded, lava strewn bottom. Every time I surfaced, I found myself further from shore and closer to lava formations protruding from the water. Razor sharp, I knew if I got thrown against them, I'd be cut to pieces.

I swam even harder.

As waves continued to pour over me, I felt like I'd been caught in a washing machine. I'd surface for a few seconds, gasping for air before being thrust downward into the lava studded bottom. Nothing was spared. My whole body became raked. Within moments, I knew I would hit the outcropping of lava. What if I hit my head or got knocked out? I felt drained of energy. I envisioned myself being thrown against the rocks until I couldn't stay above water.

Don't panic! If you panic, you'll drown!

At first, my pride had kept me from calling out. I was an experienced swimmer. I was strong. But now, I feared for my life.

"Help! Help me!" I called loud as I could. Bobbing, I could see surfers on the far side of the beach. They were about 200 yards away; too far to hear.

I'd nearly reached the rock formations. I was tired. I felt spent. I struggled to get myself away. Despite my best intentions, panic set in.

Dear God, help me! I'm too young to die!

... ...

I'd grown up in a small town in Indiana. Like many, I became the product of a broken home. Though I didn't know it at the time, my father had issues with drugs and alcohol, disappearing for weeks at a time. Soon after, the physical abuse began. By the time I'd entered kindergarten, my parents had divorced. I rarely saw him after that.

At a young age I began to isolate myself; partly due to the abuse as well as feelings of abandonment. It didn't help I became the target of ridicule from kids at school. As one of the youngest of many siblings, I often wore hand-me-downs. While classmates were wearing eighties jeans, I wore orange bell bottoms from the seventies.

I'd watch shows on television, and then try to emulate their stylish fashions. In a rural community, trendy urban styles don't easily mix. Classmates often made fun of me. As a result, I became a loner. I didn't make friends and my isolation grew. As one of the youngest, my older siblings often took out their frustrations on me.

Mom did the best she could making sure we had a Christian upbringing. We attended various churches and remained active at times, but it never seemed to last. No matter the worship, I hadn't experienced a single denomination where I felt any kinship.

I'd always believed in a God of some form or another. In my heart, I knew there had to be. But I didn't know Him. I didn't feel that He was for me. If I didn't fit in with my own family, how could I fit into the family of God?

I knew right from wrong. But as far as religion was concerned, I felt spiritually confused. I didn't know what to believe. I didn't even know how to believe. It says in Romans 3:4 *"every man is a liar,"* so who could I believe? Could religion be a manmade thing?

It wasn't until I became an adult that I realized why I felt different from everyone else. I'd begun to make new friends in another city. Some of them identified themselves as gay. After a conversation with one who explained how he came to that realization, I questioned my own identity.

I had *never* considered myself gay. In fact, I didn't want to be gay! I'd been taught it was wrong. Gays were dirty and dark; they lie, steal and cheat.

Maybe I'm gay!

Who would want that? I recalled my isolation, the name calling and a lifetime struggling to fit in. And, if people thought so poorly of them, what would God think of me? If I was rejected in this world, wouldn't I be rejected in the world to come?

Despite my doubts, I *had* experienced something otherworldly. While visiting my sister in Georgia, something had awakened me in the middle of the night. Unable to go back to sleep, I decided to get up. I went outside intending to light a cigarette. It was December, and cold.

I happened to look upward.

What at first seemed like a glowing speck, grew larger until it became this gorgeous, flowing, white light. It didn't have a face or a body. It was just this glowing, wispy mass of light. It came toward me, stopping a few feet away. Though it was white-like, it wasn't a light as you see through human eyes. It was warm and glowing. It flowed with a substance I can only compare with yards and yards of chiffon. It undulated before me.

It was beautiful! It was heavenly. I knew it had to be an angel. I didn't hear spoken words, but a message came into my heart. I felt it in my guts. *You need to go now. Get to Louisville as fast as you can. You need to be with Carol. Move now!*

Carol was my childhood friend. We'd been sweethearts in school. This wasn't a warm and fuzzy feeling. It felt fearful. All I could think about was what I needed to do. I had to go!

I immediately woke my sister, apologizing about my departure before jumping into the car around three a.m. I drove through the night and the next day, arriving in Kentucky the following evening.

I'd only been at Carol's for two hours when I heard someone enter the kitchen back door. Louisville is hilly. So even if the front porch had a few steps, the house could be built into a hill. Whoever it was, had to climb two flights of stairs instead of entering in front at ground level. Carol was preparing a meal in the kitchen.

All at once, I heard heated arguing. It sounded like Ted, Carol's husband. Something in his voice made me rush to the kitchen. With her back against the cupboard, her husband held a butcher knife and it was pointed at her face. When he saw me standing there, he dropped the knife and ran out the door.

Maybe he ran because he wasn't expecting anyone else to be there. Maybe he ran because he stood five feet two inches tall, and I was six foot two. Most likely, he knew if he ever hurt her, he'd have to deal with me.

Carol broke the silence. "He was high on meth."

I suddenly understood. If I hadn't been there; if I hadn't left in the middle of the night, it would've been too late.

And though I'd never joined a church, it seemed God could still *use* me. My trip had turned into a very spiritual experience. I had just come from a revival before visiting my sister. Once there, I had an encounter with an angel who sent me on a mission. And on the way back home, I got baptized in a Florida swamp by a friend.

I didn't have all the answers, but I knew there was more about God I wanted to know.

Years later, while living in Seattle, I'd developed a friendship with two sisters, Laura and Sally. They were caring for their mother in her final weeks with Alzheimer's. I began visiting. We discovered she didn't slip into dementia as much while telling me stories of her life in Maui. She seemed in a better frame of mind, a better mood. I began coming over more often, running errands, helping them cook and clean. We grew very fond of each other before her passing.

Afterward, I went to help Laura renovate their rental house in Maui. I readily agreed even though it meant ripping up carpet and deep cleaning. I hadn't had a vacation in a really long time. Sun, sand and water sounded wonderful. Originally intended as a two week working vacation; it evolved into six, with all my free time spent at the beach.

That particular day in May was no different. I carpooled to the ocean, and then walked past Big Beach to get to Little Beach. Though the waves were high, it was a beautiful day for bodysurfing. I dove in, enjoying the water. All at once, I became upended by a large wave. My idyllic day had spun into nightmare.

"Help! Help me!"

My voice sounded weak. Surely, no one heard. And even if they did, they were too far away. Scattered thoughts crossed my mind like a drumbeat. *Dear God! Help me! I'm not ready to die! Dear God! Help me! I'm not ready to die!*

"Help me! Somebody help me!" I called for a third time.

All at once, a figure appeared to my right. It was a boy about fifteen years old, kneeling on a French blue surfboard. He had blue eyes and shoulder length blond hair. And, even though he appeared to be a surfer dude, he wasn't tanned by the sun.

"Help me!" I screamed as my mind flooded with intense thankfulness. *Thank God somebody was nearby!*

He paddled right over to me, saying, "Grab onto my surfboard and kick!"

I grabbed onto his board with my left hand. As he paddled, I began a mantra in my mind. *Kick! Kick! Kick! Kick! Kick! Kick! Kick!* No words were spoken between us. He paddled. I kicked.

We were heading toward shore at an angle, and not straight toward it, like I'd been trying to swim. I was on the seaward side of his board, so those standing on the beach would've had trouble seeing me.

Time seemed to disappear. I had no sense of how long I'd been kicking or how long it took us to near the shore. Once we reached the shallows, the surfer boy said, "Swim on a *diagonal*. Once your feet hit the sand, go straight for the beach."

By now, I was exhausted but did exactly as he bid. I made it, walking a few steps before collapsing on the sand. Those who'd been watching ran up and surrounded me.

"Oh my God! We thought you were a goner!" a woman said.

"Are you okay? Do you need an ambulance?" said another.

As I lay there, I had difficulty understanding their words. Sure, I was tired, but an ambulance? "Why?" I asked, finally.

"Because you're covered in blood."

I looked at myself for the first time. Cuts covered my body, and they bled profusely. But I was alive! "No, no, no. I'm fine," I said, sitting up. "I just want to thank that surfer boy for saving my life."

"*What* surfer boy?"

"The one who came over and got me," I said. "The one who had me grab his surfboard and told me to kick."

"There wasn't anyone else," said a third.

"You *had* to see him. I want to thank that boy who saved my life!"

Everyone insisted that there had been no one else. I'd been alone the whole time. But, I was so sure they were wrong that for the next hour I walked up and down the beach, searching for him. I knew I'd spot him, for his surfboard was *French* blue which happened to be my favorite color. I even went to the other end of the beach, watching as each surfer came to shore. He wasn't among them. Next, I began counting surfers, thinking I'd missed him somehow. Though I rinsed off a few times with saltwater, I continued to bleed until bandaged later that day.

I never found him. But I continued to believe he was *real*.

It wasn't until years later; I finally realized my surfer boy must have been an angel. I'd only believed in angels like those depicted in paintings because I had once witnessed one.

They were beautiful and full of light. They came from the sky. They came to give messages. I didn't realize they could also come in human form.

The most pressing thing I'd learned through my experience was that God is real. All doubt had been swept away with the rip current. Before, I took life for granted. Life was now precious to me. I knew it could be taken at any moment. It also put a sense in me that I had some level of importance. Why was I spared? There had to be a reason. It created a strong faith which I now pursue.

It also reaffirmed there was something beyond a specific church or religion.

God didn't wait until I'd professed a particular faith to save me. Whatever God was, He was *Spirit*. That, I could believe in. I might be confused about religion because I've been told there's a right way to worship and believe in God and there's a wrong way. But, I knew I could worship God in Spirit and never be wrong.

Different religions, different denominations are often at odds with each other. Most people believe theirs is the true religion. Yet, I don't feel the need to worry about *religion;* which religion is right or which is wrong. I don't need to worry what's right for one person and what's wrong for another. The common denominator for them all is the Holy Spirit and that Christ died for our sins. God is the great equalizer. Whatever religion it takes for you to get to and understand God's Spirit, that's which church you should attend.

Like a racer who jumps hurdles. Life creates different hurdles for people to jump. Some can jump four foot hurdles, others can only manage those lower to the ground. I've come to accept my hurdles. I know I will run my race with the help of God.

I'm like the Samaritan woman who Jesus met at the well. (John 4: 1-42) Jesus was resting from a journey and sat by a well near Samaria. It was noon, and his disciples had gone into a nearby town. When the woman arrived to draw water, Jesus asked her for a drink.

"You are a Jew and I am a Samaritan woman. How can you ask me for a drink?" For Jews did not associate with Samaritans. (They were considered half-breeds; dirty.)

Jesus answered her, "If you knew the gift of God and who is it that asks you for a drink, you would have asked him and he would have given you living water."

"Sir," the woman said, "you have nothing to draw with and the well is deep. Where can you get this living water? Are you greater than our father Jacob, who gave us the well and drank from it himself, as did also his sons and his livestock?"

Jesus answered, "Everyone who drinks this water will be thirsty again, but whoever drinks the water I give them will never thirst. Indeed, the water I give them will become in them a spring of water welling up to eternal life."

As a child I always felt inferior. I never had the model childhood with a mom and dad. I came from a broken home, a broken family. I always felt substandard. Like a substandard human. And, because I'd always been taught being gay was bad and wrong; I felt unwanted.

Like a Samaritan.

If Jesus could break Jewish law for the Samaritan woman, he could do so for me. He is the son of God. He *is* the law. Though she was despised by everyone, she was still accepted at God's well.

I now have a sense of belonging. Not only does God have room for a lot of people, he also has room for me. Since my experience, my values have really changed. Salvation means no one is any better or any less than anyone else. It's not for me to judge who's more important than anyone. We all have equal value in one way or another. We're all unique individuals. It's clear to me there is a spirit world and there is something on the other side. And that it's for everybody; not just for some select people. It's for everybody.

There is something out there greater than us. It is God. And, He's shown I'm accepted as I am.

"All those the Father gives me will come to me, and whoever comes to me I will never drive away." John 6:37

"I delight greatly in the Lord; my soul rejoices in my God. For He has clothed me with garments of salvation and arrayed me in a robe of righteousness, as a bridegroom adorns his head like a priest, and as a bride adorns herself with jewels." Isaiah 61:10

Jay Kline
Decatur, Indiana

About the Author

Monica lives on an Indiana farm with her husband, two of her four children, a dog and a barn cat. Before writing her first book she worked twenty-five years in the medical field of optometry. During that time she wrote a human interest story in a medical newsletter and has had poetry published in *Speer Presents*. She's written two historical romance novels *Threads of Betrayal* and the sequel *Winds of Betrayal*. Her next novel *Sons of Betrayal* will round out the trilogy.

Author Request

If you have experienced a spiritual experience that changed your life and are interested in sharing it with others, please contact me.

Postscript

Thank you for reading *Spiritual Experiences and Revelations*. If you enjoyed the book, I hope you'll consider leaving a review at: Amazon.com.

This book is also available at Createspace.com and other major retailers.

In addition to writing, I offer an author presentation titled: *One Writer's Journey/Lessons in Perseverance* to any group/club/library interested in having a guest speaker. If you'd like having me as a guest speaker, it would be my pleasure to see if I can accommodate you.

Please contact me at: www.monicakoldykemiller.com, monicarendell@hotmail.com, or Facebook/Monica Young Miller

Made in the USA
Columbia, SC
16 October 2018